W9-ALM-496

The Byzantine Empire

Other titles in the World History Series

Ancient Greece

The Early Middle Ages

Elizabethan England

The Late Middle Ages

The Nuremberg Trials

The Relocation of the North American Indian

The Roman Empire

The Roman Republic

The Byzantine Empire

James A. Corrick

LUCENT BOOKS

An imprint of Thomson Gale, a part of The Thomson Corporation

THOMSON

™

GALE

949.5
COR

Detroit • New York • San Francisco • San Diego • New Haven, Conn. • Waterville, Maine • London • Munich

For more information, contact
Lucent Books
27500 Drake Rd.
Farmington Hills, MI 48331-3535
Or you can visit our Internet site at http://www.gale.com

LIBRARY OF CONGRESS CATALOGING-IN-PUBLICATION DATA

Corrick, James A.
    The Byzantine Empire / by James A. Corrick
        p. cm. — (World history series)
Includes bibliographical references and index.
ISBN 1-59018-837-3
1. Byzantine Empire—Civilization—Juvenile literature. I. Title. II. Series.
DF552.C67 2006
949.5'02—dc22

2005023729

Printed in the United States of America

Contents

Foreword   6

Important Dates During the Byzantine Empire   8

Introduction:
Heirs to the Roman Empire   10

Chapter One:
From Rome to Byzantium   14

Chapter Two:
Shaping the Empire: The Law and the Sword   24

Chapter Three:
The Byzantine Church and State   37

Chapter Four:
The Flowering of Byzantine Culture   49

Chapter Five:
Threats from Without: The Armies of Persia and Islam   59

Chapter Six:
Threats from Within: Heretics and Landlords   68

Chapter Seven:
Crusaders and Turks   78

Notes   90

For Further Reading   92

Works Consulted   95

Index   99

Picture Credits   103

About the Author   104

Foreword

Each year, on the first day of school, nearly every history teacher faces the task of explaining why his or her students should study history. Many reasons have been given. One is that lessons exist in the past from which contemporary society can benefit and learn. Another is that exploration of the past allows us to see the origins of our customs, ideas, and institutions. Concepts such as democracy, ethnic conflict, or even things as trivial as fashion or mores, have historical roots.

Reasons such as these impress few students, however. If anything, these explanations seem remote and dull to young minds. Yet history is anything but dull. And therein lies what is perhaps the most compelling reason for studying history: History is filled with great stories. The classic themes of literature and drama—love and sacrifice, hatred and revenge, injustice and betrayal, adversity and overcoming adversity—fill the pages of history books, feeding the imagination as well as any of the great works of fiction do.

The story of the Children's Crusade, for example, is one of the most tragic in history. In 1212 Crusader fever hit Europe. A call went out from the pope that all good Christians should journey to Jerusalem to drive out the hated Muslims and return the city to Christian control. Heeding the call, thousands of children made the jour-

ney. Parents bravely allowed many children to go, and entire communities were inspired by the faith of these small Crusaders. Unfortunately, many boarded ships captained by slave traders, who enthusiastically sold the children into slavery as soon as they arrived at their destination. Thousands died from disease, exposure, and starvation on the long march across Europe to the Mediterranean Sea. Others perished at sea.

Another story, from a modern and more familiar place, offers a soul-wrenching view of personal humiliation but also the ability to rise above it. Hatsuye Egami was one of 110,000 Japanese Americans sent to internment camps during World War II. "Since yesterday we Japanese have ceased to be human beings," he wrote in his diary. "We are numbers. We are no longer Egamis, but the number 23324. A tag with that number is on every trunk, suitcase and bag. Tags, also, on our breasts." Despite such dehumanizing treatment, most internees worked hard to control their bitterness. They created workable communities inside the camps and demonstrated again and again their loyalty as Americans.

These are but two of the many stories from history that can be found in the pages of the Lucent Books World History series. All World History titles rely on sound research and verifiable evidence, and all give students a clear sense of time, place, and chronology through maps and time-lines as well as text.

All titles include a wide range of author-itative perspectives that demonstrate the complexity of historical interpretation and sharpen the reader's critical thinking skills. Formally documented quotations and annotated bibliographies enable students to locate and evaluate sources, often instantaneously via the Internet, and serve as valuable tools for further research and debate.

Finally, Lucent's World History titles present rousing good stories, featuring vivid primary source quotations drawn from unique, sometimes obscure sources such as diaries, public records, and con-temporary chronicles. In this way, the voices of participants and witnesses as well as important biographers and histo-rians bring the study of history to life. As we are caught up in the lives of others, we are reminded that we too are characters in the ongoing human saga, and we are better prepared for our own roles.

Important Dates During

330
Constantine I founds Constantinople.

529
The Code of Justinian replaces the old Byzantine legal code.

713
Kojiki, the first history of Japan, appears.

476
The Western Roman Empire falls, and the Eastern rises as the Byzantine Empire.

554
The Byzantine Empire reaches its greatest geographical extent.

| 300 | 400 | 500 | 600 | 700 | 800 |

635
Muslim armies begin their assault on the Byzantine Empire.

ca. 520
An Indian Buddhist monk, Bodhidharma, develops Zen.

ca. 600
The Mayan city Tikal becomes the largest urban center in the Americas.

538
Koreans bring Buddhism to Japan.

the Byzantine Empire

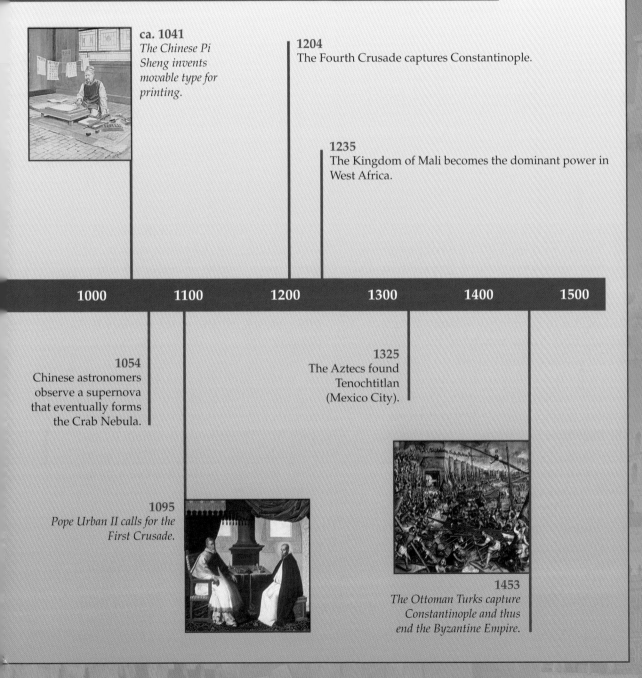

ca. 1041
The Chinese Pi Sheng invents movable type for printing.

1204
The Fourth Crusade captures Constantinople.

1235
The Kingdom of Mali becomes the dominant power in West Africa.

1000	1100	1200	1300	1400	1500

1054
Chinese astronomers observe a supernova that eventually forms the Crab Nebula.

1325
The Aztecs found Tenochtitlan (Mexico City).

1095
Pope Urban II calls for the First Crusade.

1453
The Ottoman Turks capture Constantinople and thus end the Byzantine Empire.

Heirs to the Roman Empire

In A.D. 476 the emperor of the Western Roman Empire, Romulus Augustulus, was overthrown, and the first in a series of non-Roman, Germanic kings took his place. This event is usually given as the fall of the once-mighty Roman Empire, which had ruled much of the known world for five hundred years. However, this imperial collapse affected only the western section of the empire. The Eastern Roman Empire survived, and thrived, as the Byzantine Empire throughout the Middle Ages, the thousand-year period of European history from the fall of Rome to the Renaissance in the 1400s.

The stability and longevity of the Byzantine Empire can be credited to several factors. According to historian George Ostrogorsky:

The Byzantine state had at its disposal a unique administrative machine with a highly differentiated and well-trained civil service, its military technique was superb, and it possessed an excellent legal system and was based on a highly developed economic and financial system. It commanded great wealth [in contrast to other states of] the early medieval period.[1]

Thus, while barbarian warlords fought each other and struggled to create kingdoms out of the shattered Western Roman Empire, the Byzantines flourished, and their state became a center of art and learning and Europe's main defense against invasion from Asia.

From Roman to Greek to Byzantine

Throughout their history the Byzantines continued to call themselves Romans because they continued to think of their realm as the Roman Empire. In the same spirit the Byzantine leaders believed that they were the direct heirs of the emperors of Rome. These claims have led some modern historians to dub the Byzantine state the Later Roman Empire. The label Byzantine, by which the era and society are best known today, was not used then in either the East or West; the term was introduced by sixteenth-century German historian Hieronymus Wolf and not popularized until the 1700s.

The name Later Roman Empire is apt because the Byzantines did inherit much from Rome. Like Rome, they had an imperial bureaucracy overseen by an emperor and a senate. Importantly, like Rome—at least since A.D. 389—the Byzantine state was Christian. Certain Byzantine cultural traditions and enthusiasms, such as chariot racing, also came from Rome.

Yet there was much about the empire that was not Roman. For instance, by the sixth century the toga, the symbol of the Roman ruling class, had been replaced by silk coats, and men wore beards rather than went clean-shaven as had ancient Romans. Also, far more than the old Roman emperors, Byzantine emperors' rule was marked by elaborate ritual. Further, Greek replaced Latin as the official language of the empire.

As a consequence of these and other differences and notwithstanding Byzantine claims, western Europeans of the Middle Ages always viewed the empire as Greek, not Roman, and largely foreign.

Constantinople

Some eastern and western Europeans, however, did call the empire Byzantium, from an ancient name for the Byzantine

The sport of chariot racing, which is depicted in this Byzantine carving, was a holdover from the Roman Empire.

capital, Constantinople. Named for the Roman emperor Constantine I, who founded the city in the fourth century A.D., Constantinople was built on the site of an earlier Greek settlement. The name of the Greek town's legendary founder was Byzas, from which came Byzantium.

Constantinople was not only the political heart of the Byzantine Empire but also the center of Byzantine trade. Its pivotal location guaranteed its commercial dominance. The city sat on the European side of the Bosporus, the narrow strait that links the Black Sea, via the Sea of Marmara and the Dardanelles, to the Aegean Sea in the Mediterranean and essentially connects Europe to Asia. Positioned so, Constantinople was able to control trade moving north and south through the Bosporus and east and west across it. The empire grew rich on this trade.

Cultural Storehouse

The importance of the Byzantine Empire in shaping European civilization, however, went far beyond trade. A crucial role of the empire was to preserve the ancient Greek and Roman literature, philosophy, and political history upon which modern Western civilization is based. In Europe the classical writings of Aristotle, Plato, Sophocles, and many others were mostly destroyed in the warfare that preceded and followed the fall of Rome, but these works remained safe in Byzantine libraries. Ostrogorsky remarks that "rooted in the Greek tradition, Byzantium stood for a thousand years as the most important stronghold of culture and learning . . . in the medieval world."[2]

Arabic translations (and Greek and Latin texts) of these preserved works would eventually reach western Europe when the empire expanded into Spain and Sicily during the later Middle Ages. Byzantine teachers and scholars immigrating to Italy also brought copies with them. The rediscovery and study of these ancient texts contributed to the flowering of culture and knowledge known as the Renaissance.

Defender of Europe

The second important role played by the Byzantine Empire was as a buffer against potential invasion of western Europe from the East. Western rulers were relatively weak and disorganized for five centuries following the fall of the Western Roman Empire, preoccupied with wars against barbarian northern tribes and vulnerable to invasion. However, eastern invaders generally targeted the Byzantine Empire instead. The empire, rich in both treasure and culture, was a more valuable and tempting prize for would-be conquerors.

During the early Middle Ages particularly, the Byzantines repelled Persian and Muslim invasions, and they fought against various nomadic tribes who came out of central Asia. True, some invaders, such as the Bulgars, Avars, and Magyars, did conquer parts of eastern Europe. However, successful Byzantine resistance kept the intruders from turning their full attention toward western Europe, since they exhausted their resources and warriors in battle with the Byzantines. As the scholar Will Durant writes, "Avars, Persians, Arabs, [and Bulgarians] would threaten . . . in turn and

The Byzantine Empire served as a buffer between Europe and invaders from the East. In this illustration, Byzantine soldiers battle Arab forces.

fail."[3] Thus, the still struggling and young western kingdoms were well enough shielded by the Byzantines to survive and grow, finally evolving into the nations of western Europe. But before the empire could become an effective barrier to Europe, it had to survive the onslaught of the first wave of invaders—German barbarians.

Chapter One

From Rome to Byzantium

The emergence of the Byzantine Empire from the crumbling Roman Empire took about a century and a half. During that time the western part of the Roman Empire collapsed under the weight of its internal problems and the attacks of its external enemies. The eastern portion, which would become the Byzantine Empire, weathered this period of crisis, remaining relatively stable and geographically intact.

New Rome

The Byzantine Empire actually originated in A.D. 330 when Constantine I, emperor of a Roman Empire that stretched from Britain to the Middle East, dedicated the city of Constantinople, or as he called it, New Rome. The dedication date, May 11, became an important holiday in the Byzantine calendar.

Constantinople covered a triangular peninsula connected to the mainland on its west side, where Constantine had a wall built to block attacks by land. To the south of the city was the Sea of Marmara, to the east, the Bosporus, and to the north, the Golden Horn. The latter was a long, narrow body of water that looked like a horn or a crooked finger. It stretched inland from the Bosporus and was the city's harbor.

After the new city's completion, Constantine moved the imperial capital from Rome to Constantinople. An important reason for this move was political turmoil in Rome. The Italian city was full of battling political parties, many of whom traced their history back centuries to the old Roman Republic. Some of these parties wanted to strengthen imperial authority, while others wanted to limit the emperor's authority or abolish imperial rule altogether and restore the old republican form of government. Civil unrest was common and civil war possible in the political hotbed of Rome, all risks that made the old capital a dangerous place for the emperor.

The City

As the political center of the Roman Empire, Constantinople's population and importance grew rapidly over the next decades. Indeed, within a century Constantinople resembled large modern cities in terms of size and population. No European city would rival it for a thousand years. Not even once-splendid Rome could compare to the eastern capital. According to Durant, Constantinople had nearly a million inhabitants and was an architectural showplace: "An official document (c.450) lists five imperial palaces, six palaces for the ladies of the court, three for high dignitaries, 4,388 mansions, 322 streets, 53 porticoes, add to these a thousand shops, a hundred places of amusement, sumptuous baths, brilliantly ornamented churches, and magnificent squares."[4] In recognition of its unique status, Constantinople was called simply the City. Its modern name, Istanbul, is actually a distortion of the Greek phrase "to the city."

The old imperial capital, Rome, by contrast, suffered through hard times. Its population declined, and its public buildings and monuments fell apart from lack of money to repair and maintain them. Rome was no longer even an Italian administrative center, Milan having taken over that function.

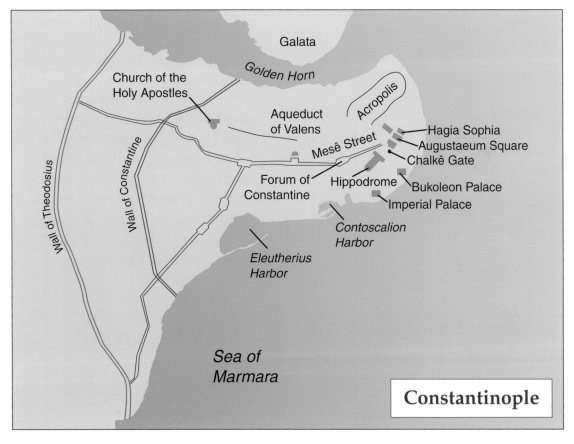

Constantinople

Constantine's City

In his Byzantine Civilization *historian Steven Runciman describes the mixed character of Emperor Constantine's new capital, Constantinople.*

"Constantinople was set on Greek-speaking coasts and incorporated an old Greek city. But Constantine did more to emphasize its Hellenism. His capital was to be the center of art and learning. He built libraries stocked with Greek manuscripts; still more, he filled its streets and squares and museums with art treasures drawn from all over the Greek world. The citizen of Constantinople could never forget the glory of his Hellenic heritage.

But it was a Roman city too. For over two centuries the [imperial] Court and a large proportion of the inhabitants were Latin-speaking; and Latin was still the educated language of the Balkan hinterland. . . . Constantine gave the city mob the privilege of free bread and free [gladiatorial contests and chariot-racing] that the poor of Rome enjoyed; and the upper classes were induced, according to legend, to transplant themselves to the Bosporus by the gift of palaces that exactly reproduced their Roman homes. Constantinople was to be another Rome.

The third element was the Christian East. Constantinople was to be a Christian city. The [non-Christian] temples of old Byzantium were allowed to stand a little longer, and it seems that some were even put up for the benefit of pagans engaged in constructing the city. But after the work was finished, no more were to be built."

The Emperor Constantine, shown in this Renaissance tapestry by Peter Paul Rubens, built the Byzantine capital on Greek and Roman cultural foundations.

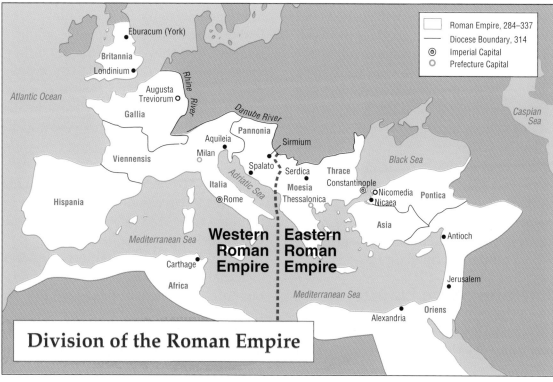

Division of the Roman Empire

Division of Empire

Even from the new capital, administering a sprawling, besieged empire proved too much for Constantine and his successors. In 364 Emperor Valentinian I divided the Roman Empire into western and eastern sections to be ruled by two coemperors, Valentinian in the west and his brother Valens in the east. Constantinople was the eastern capital, Milan the western. Later, the naval port of Ravenna on Italy's Adriatic coast became the western capital.

The division was a practical solution to the problems of managing the immense territory of the Roman Empire. The empire at this time covered an area larger than the continental United States and stretched from the Atlantic Ocean in the west to the Persian Gulf in the east, a distance equal to that between New York City and Los Angeles in a time without modern communication or transportation. It could take months—sometimes years—for commands to reach every region of the empire.

East and West

Valentinian divided the empire between its Greek-speaking (Byzantine) eastern and the Latin-speaking (Roman) western territories. The Byzantine division comprised the Balkan Peninsula, Asia Minor, the Middle East, and Egypt; the western territory consisted of Italy, Spain, Gaul (roughly equal to present-day France), Britain, and the western half of North Africa.

In theory the Roman empire was still a single entity, but in reality the two sections functioned quite independently of each other, and the disagreements and differences between them deepened over time. The split was not good for the western division because it had a smaller population and less wealth than its eastern partner. Also, the western area was less compact and thus not as easily governed as the eastern territories. Scholar David Nicholas writes that "population density and per-capita wealth were much higher in the east than in the west, making it less difficult to support the [imperial government]. . . . The eastern empire was more easily governable, centered on Asia Minor with a centrally located capital."[5]

Enemies of the Empire

The Roman Empire's internal problems were complicated by external threats. To the east was the aggressive Persian Empire. Over the next century the Romans and Persians would fight a series of wars that caused much bloodshed but little overall change in the balance of power between the two states.

The second threat to the empire came from tribes of German barbarians living north of the Danube, which was the empire's northern border in the east. These barbarians launched constant raids across the border. Occasionally, Roman armies crossed the Danube and fought pitched battles with the Germans. Until the late fourth century the empire managed to confine major clashes, as well as large German forces, to lands north of the Danube.

German Immigrants

The imperial governments, however, had no objection to individual Germans or small family groups entering and settling in imperial territory. In small numbers the barbarians posed no threat to the empire's security, and they proved useful, filling necessary jobs on farms and in the army's ranks.

The chief risk was actually borne by the immigrating Germans, who were not eligible for Roman citizenship and who were subject to mistreatment by imperial officials and citizens. It was not unusual for Germans to have their property stolen or for them to be sold into slavery. Still, the Germans kept coming because they saw the empire as a land of opportunity, and eventually, they were scattered throughout both the eastern and western Roman Empire.

Soldiering was the most popular profession of the German immigrants. By the fourth century the imperial armies were made up mostly of mercenaries, with the Germans supplying the bulk of these troops. Thus, by the early 400s both the Byzantine and western armies of the Roman Empire were filled with Germans, a number of whom even rose to the rank of general.

The Visigoths

The first significant German incursion occurred in 376 when some sixty thousand Visigoths, or West Goths, moved south across the Danube and into the eastern Roman Empire. The Goths were not invaders since they had received the Byzantine emperor's permission to settle on imperial land. However, after government officials stole from them, sold their children into slavery, and tried to kill their leader, the Goths became a hostile army that ravaged the countryside. At Adrianople in 378 an imperial army sent to stop the barbarians' rampage was defeated and the Byzantine emperor Valens killed. This defeat and Valens's death shocked and frightened imperial citizens in both sections of the empire.

However great the Visigoths' victory at Adrianople, they did not go on to conquer the Eastern Roman Empire in the fourth century. Although they attacked Constantinople, they lacked the force needed to break through the city's excellent defenses. Eventually, after plundering the Balkans, the Goths turned west, where they struck a deal with the Western Roman emperor, who allowed them to settle in imperial territory. In time, just as with the

This engraving depicts the conquest of Rome by the Visigoths in A.D. 410.

Eastern Empire, the barbarians had a falling out with the Western Empire, and in 410 they attacked and looted Rome, then left Italy for Spain.

The news of the plundering of Rome shocked the citizens of the Eastern Empire even more than the defeat at Adrianople. In Constantinople the news prompted sixteen thousand volunteers to build a massive new city wall, which according to writer L. Sprague de Camp, was "13 to 15 feet [4 to 4.5m] thick, 30 to 40 feet [9 to 12m] high, and 4.5 miles [7km] long, with ninety-six towers."[6] Later, across the mouth of the Golden Horn, city officials stretched a chain that could be raised or lowered to keep out enemy ships. Such measures ensured the city's survival during the many sieges that it endured over the next thousand years. Indeed, the city proved to be one of the world's great fortresses, its defenses and defenders turning back one group of invaders after another.

Crumbling Defenses

No matter how well defended Constantinople was, the Roman Empire in general was not. After the Visigoths' campaign the imperial defenses crumbled, and one

The Visigoths Arrive

The fourth-century historian Ammianus Marcellinus gives the following account of the Visigoths' arrival in the eastern Roman Empire in his Roman History.

"Under the command of their leader Alavivus, [the Visigoths] occupied the banks of the Danube, and sent ambassadors to the Emperor Valens, humbly entreating to be received by him as his subjects. They promised to live quietly, and to furnish a body of [troops].

The affair seemed a cause of joy rather than of fear, according to the skillful flatterers who were always extolling and exaggerating the good fortune of the emperor. They congratulated him that an embassy had come from the farthest corners of the earth, unexpectedly offering him a large body of recruits; and that, by combining the strength of his own people with these foreign forces, he would have an army absolutely invincible; observing further that the payment for military reinforcements, which came in every year from the provinces, a vast treasure of gold might now be saved and accumulated in his coffers.

Full of this hope, [the emperor] sent forth several officers to bring this ferocious people and their carts into our territory, [and] no one was left behind, not even of those who were stricken with mortal disease."

barbarian army after another made its way into the empire. These invasions succeeded for several reasons. First, Germans who had traded and soldiered in the empire spread detailed reports about imperial defenses, troop positions, and tactics to their fellows outside the empire.

Second, the armies in both the Western and Eastern Roman Empires lacked the manpower and organization to protect the long imperial borders. Recruitment plunged along with the general decline in population caused by a series of plagues in the third and fourth centuries. Even with the addition of mercenaries, troop levels fell below that required to repel invasion.

Finally, Roman leadership during this period was generally poor. In both the Western and Eastern Empires weak and incompetent emperors ruled, and imperial officials frequently diverted money meant for the armies into their own purses. Additionally, when strong leaders did appear they were assassinated by political rivals who feared their growing power.

The end result of all these imperial weaknesses was that various German invaders seized Western territory piece by piece until little was left of the Western Roman Empire except Italy. Historian Crane Brinton observes that "the eastern portion of the Empire . . . usually managed to deflect the new blows of further invaders so that they fell chiefly upon the West." Thus, Brinton concludes, despite continuing barbarian attacks, including a frightening but unsuccessful invasion by the Huns, led by Attila, in the mid-fifth century, "the cities of the East continued prosperous, and government operated undisturbed."[7]

One Emperor Again

In 476 a non-Roman, the barbarian Odoacer, overthrew the last Western Roman emperor Romulus Augustulus. Odoacer then struck a bargain with the newly crowned Eastern Roman emperor Zeno. The barbarian would recognize Zeno's authority as sole ruler of the Roman Empire. In exchange Zeno would appoint Odoacer imperial governor of Italy.

Today, Odoacer's assumption of power is widely cited as the date marking the fall of the Roman Empire. At the time, however, no one in the West or the East viewed the new development that way. Under Odoacer life in Italy continued much as it had. As Durant writes: "No one seems to have seen in this event the 'fall of Rome'; on the contrary, it seemed to be a blessed unification of the Empire. . . . The Roman Senate saw the matter so, and raised a statue to Zeno. The Germanization of the Italian army, government, and peasantry seemed to be negligible shifts on the surface of the national scene."[8]

Still, although in theory the Eastern emperor was now sole ruler of the Roman Empire, in practice he had limited authority in the Western section. In recognition of this fact many modern historians view the post-476 Eastern Roman Empire as a new state, the Byzantine Empire.

The Ostrogoths

Although Odoacer governed Italy well, he was too independent to suit Zeno. The emperor complained that he had lost

Eastern Survival

The scholar Michael Grant in his History of Rome *explains some of the reasons why the Byzantine Empire survived while its western counterpart did not.*

"The western empire was far more vulnerable to external attack owing to its geographical location. In Europe, it had to guard the long frontiers of the Upper and Middle Danube and the Rhine whereas the Byzantine Empire had only the Lower Danube to cover. . . . If the western emperor failed to hold his river barriers, he had no second line of defense to fall back upon, and Italy and Gaul and Spain lay wide open to the invaders; whereas to force the Bosporus, guarded by the impregnable defenses of Constantinople, was beyond the capacity of any hostile power.

Furthermore, the eastern empire possessed a sounder social and economic structure than the western. . . . In contrast to the West, the middle class, the traditional nucleus of ancient society, survived . . . in tolerable economic conditions; and employing this class to man a professional civil service that was more effective than its western counterpart, the Byzantine authorities managed to gather in a much higher proportion of the national income than the court of Ravenna was ever able to collect.

Furthermore, the internal political stability of the eastern empire was far more impressive. During a whole century and a half from A.D. 365, its internal peace was broken only by five usurpers (three of them in the same reign), a remarkable contrast to the proliferation of such rebels in the west."

control of Italy because Odoacer was acting like an independent ruler, not a governor answerable to the emperor. For Zeno the only way to restore imperial authority in the west was to remove Odoacer.

At the same time, Zeno was facing a problem closer to home. Settled in the upper Balkans was a tribe of Germans, the Ostrogoths, or East Goths. Although the Ostrogoths had pledged their loyalty to the empire, they occasionally raided their imperial neighbors to the south, a nuisance that threatened to destabilize the region.

Zeno decided that the best way to end these raids was to move the Ostrogoths out of the Balkans. Thus in 488 he invited the Ostrogoths to invade Italy and wrest control from Odoacer. The emperor believed this was a good plan because it would both remove Odoacer and rid the Byzantine Empire of the Ostrogoths. Further, Zeno felt that the leader of the Ostrogoths, Theodoric, would be more controllable than Odoacer because the Goth had been raised and educated in Constantinople. Historian Norman F. Cantor notes that "Theodoric went to Italy with the understanding that the rights of the emperor in

Italy would be preserved. The emperor considered the Ostrogothic king his lieutenant, and he expected that the Ostrogothic invasion would do nothing to decrease imperial sovereignty there, but would increase its strength."[9]

The Gothic Kingdom

Under the leadership of Theodoric the Ostrogoths captured Italy and killed Odoacer. For a time relations between the Byzantines and Theodoric were friendly, as Theodoric, now known as the Great, worked to bolster imperial control of Italy. The Goth also tried to strengthen the imperial government from within by combating the widespread corruption in the Roman civil service. He launched an ambitious program that cleaned up harbors, repaired aqueducts, and restored churches and public buildings. He even lowered taxes, one of his most popular reforms.

However, within ten years of the Ostrogothic takeover, Theodoric, like Odoacer, began operating as though Italy were his kingdom and he were its king. Despite Byzantine hopes, the empire had failed to bring Italy under imperial authority. Another generation would pass and a new emperor, Justinian I, would rule in Constantinople before the Byzantines again tried to gain control of Italy.

Chapter Two

Shaping the Empire: The Law and the Sword

Zeno and his immediate successors Anastasius I (491–518) and Justin I (518–527) were able leaders, far more competent than the emperors of the late Roman Empire. However, it would be Justin's nephew, Justinian I, who would prove to be the first great ruler of the Byzantine Empire. Justinian was a brilliant administrator. His long reign, from 527 to 565, was marked by two great achievements: the standardization of imperial law and the conquest of parts of the former Western Roman Empire.

The Peasant Emperor

Unlike most of the previous emperors, Justinian was not an aristocrat. Indeed, the emperor was born in 482 to peasant parents near Sardica, about 300 miles (423km) northwest of Constantinople. His lowly origins may explain his later approachability as emperor (though he lived as lavishly as any Byzantine ruler). The Byzantine historian and Justinian's

contemporary, Procopius, wrote that "even men of low estate and altogether obscure had complete freedom not only to come before him but to converse with him."[10]

Justinian's uncle, Justin, had been the commander of the palace guard, and when Emperor Anastasius I died in 518, he campaigned successfully to be named the new Byzantine ruler. Justin had already brought Justinian to Constantinople, where the latter was educated before spending several years in the army. Justin I was an old man and preferred play to work. Therefore, he put his ambitious and intelligent nephew to managing the empire. By the time Justin I died in 527, Justinian was already an experienced imperial administrator.

Justinian's experience, combined with his intelligence and his craving for hard work, made him a very capable ruler. He typically worked from dawn till late into the night. In addition to his regular duties, the emperor found time to study law, architecture, music, poetry, religion, and philosophy. Durant notes that "his mind was constantly active, equally at home in large designs and minute details."[11]

Empress Theodora

Justinian ran the empire with the valuable help of his wife and empress, Theodora.

Like her husband, Theodora was not a member of the aristocracy, her father having been a bear trainer and she herself an actress and dancer.

This common, if colorful, past did not prevent her from becoming one of the most powerful people in the Byzantine Empire. She was intelligent, witty,

Byzantine Emperor Justinian, shown in this engraving with his aides, has been called "the peasant emperor" because of his humble origins.

beautiful, and ambitious; she was also shrewd, haughty, and ruthless if necessary. Her husband recognized her political skills and made her the virtual coruler of the empire, saying that he took "as a participant in the decision [of managing the empire] my most pious consort, given me by God."[12]

The Blues and the Greens
It was Theodora who saved Justinian during the greatest crisis of his emperorship—

Empress Theodora (third from left) helped Justinian rule the Byzantine Empire.

the Nika riot of 532, when members of political factions known as the Blues and the Greens rampaged through the streets of Constantinople. At this time most citizens of the Byzantine capital belonged either to the Blues or the Greens. The former was led by the merchant class, while the latter was headed by the aristocracy. Both parties counted many from the working class as members. One faction would normally back the emperor, while the other opposed him. Occasionally, as in 532, the two parties joined together in common cause against the emperor.

The Nika Riot

The 532 uprising was sparked by Justinian's order to raise taxes. Tens of thousands of people rampaged through the city streets, killing police and other government officials and burning down many public buildings. As the rioters wrecked the city, they shouted *"Nika!"* the Greek word for "victory."

According to Procopius, only Theodora's shaming of Justinian kept him from fleeing the city and thus losing his throne. The empress reportedly announced that

> for a man who has been an Emperor to become a refugee is not to be borne. Now if you wish to save yourself, O Emperor, this is not hard. For we have much money; there is the sea, here are the boats. But think whether after you have been saved you may not come to feel that you would have preferred to die. As for me, I like a certain old proverb that says: royalty is a good shroud.[13]

Justinian stayed. First, he had one of his aides bribe the leaders of the Blues to desert the Greens. Then, the Byzantine general Belisarius trapped most of the Green rioters in a large stadium known as the Hippodrome and killed some thirty thousand of them, thus ending the riot. Such wholesale butchery did not provoke outright rebellion; such punishment for Byzantine rulers' enemies was considered normal.

Reforming the Law

The Nika riot was the low point in an otherwise very successful emperorship. For the most part, Justinian's reign was noted for its achievements rather than its failures. Foremost among these achievements was reform of the Byzantine legal code.

Imperial law was a mixture of the civic laws of Rome, the individual laws of each imperial region, rulings by judges, and imperial decrees. The code was so complex and confusing that no one could understand or consistently apply it. Justinian wanted to end this confusion and to produce a unified, official version of the code. The emperor wrote that the current code is "not within the grasp of human capacity," and thus he was led "to begin by examining what had been enacted by former and most venerated princes, to correct their constitutions [laws], and make them more easily understood."[14]

The *Code of Justinian*

Justinian appointed a famous lawyer, Tribonian, to head a commission of ten legal experts charged with a study of Byzantine law. After reportedly reading two

The Blues and the Greens

In the two excerpts below, the first quoted in L. Sprague de Camp's Great Cities of the Ancient World *and the second from the* Secret History, *the sixth-century Byzantine historian Procopius describes first the mentality of the Byzantine political factions, the Blues and the Greens, and then how some of the Blues took to setting themselves apart from the rest of the Byzantines.*

There grows up in them against their fellow men a hostility which has no cause, and at no time does it cease or disappear, for it gives place neither to the ties of marriage nor of relationship, and the case is the same even though those who differ in any respect to these colors be brothers or any other kin. They care neither for things divine nor human in these struggles.

[The Blues] revolutionized the style of wearing their hair. For they had it cut differently from the rest of the Romans: not molesting the mustache or beard, which they allowed to keep on growing as long as it would, as the Persians do, but clipping the hair short on the front of the head down to the temples, and letting it hang down in great length and disorder in the back.

The sleeves of their tunics were cut tight about the wrists, while from there to the shoulders they were of [a large] fullness; thus, whenever they moved their hands, as when applauding at the theater [or at the chariot races], these immense sleeves fluttered conspicuously.

thousand books of law, in 529 Tribonian and his fellow commissioners produced a new legal code, the *Codex Justinianus*, or the *Code of Justinian*, which replaced the previous imperial code. Later, the *Code* was expanded to include decrees by Justinian. To help law students in their study of the *Code*, Tribonian also wrote a textbook, the *Institutes*.

In addition, the commission assembled selected opinions, or rulings, of earlier Roman and Byzantine judges in the *Digest*, to be used as the basis for future judgments—an early historical example of respect for judicial precedent that became an important element of later Western law codes. Tribonian and the others were careful, however, to include only early opinions that did not challenge the authority of the emperor and to change wording in line with Justinian's purposes.

Eventually, all three of the commission's works were published as *Corpus Juris Civilis*, or the *Body of Civil Law*, still referred to today as the *Code of Justinian*. Whereas the original *Code of Justinian* had been written in Latin, the final version was written in Greek, which remained the official language of imperial law until the end of the empire in the fifteenth century.

The Nature of the *Code*

The *Code of Justinian* was in many ways a blueprint of Byzantine society. It was rooted in two concepts: First, all law comes from the emperor; second, all law must be based on orthodox—that is, officially accepted—Christianity.

The *Code* recognized the social classes of freeborn citizens and slaves and further defined citizens as either persons of rank or commoners. Although the *Code*'s provisions encouraged the freeing of slaves, it allowed desperately poor parents to sell newborn children into slavery. It created a class of serfs by ordering that any farmer who worked on a piece of land for more than thirty years was bound to that land permanently, as were his children. Serfs who left without their landlord's permission could be returned just like runaway slaves.

The *Code* did provide some protections of individual rights, particularly for women. Under Justinian's laws a woman could inherit property, and if her husband died, she could assume the guardianship of her children. Unlike men, women were no longer to be put to death for committing adultery. Rape was a capital crime, and the rapist's property was confiscated and given to his victim. Although divorce by mutual consent was not part of the *Code* until after Justinian's death, during his lifetime a wife could divorce her husband if he was unfaithful, if he accused her falsely of adultery, or if he kept her captive.

Trial and Punishment

The *Code* incorporated many legal concepts familiar to modern societies. For example, a person accused of a crime could only be thrown into prison by the order of a judge. Trials had to follow within a set time after imprisonment and be conducted by a judge appointed by the emperor. Lawyers had to swear on a

This parchment contains a portion of the Code of Justinian, which became the law of the Byzantine Empire in A.D. 529.

Bible that they would defend their clients well, while their clients had to swear that their case was just.

Defendants who were found guilty faced a host of penalties. Some punishments were monetary: A convicted person might be fined or ordered to give up all or part of his or her property. Other sentences involved harsh physical punishment. For instance, crooked tax collectors could lose a hand. Other offenders might have their noses cut off or be blinded. Various crimes called for death by beheading, crucifixion, or burning alive. Male homosexuality was punishable by death after torture, mutilation, and public display; female homosexuality, however, was ignored by the *Code.*

Justinian's *Code* eventually became the model for other European legal systems. For this reason, the scholar Aikaterina Christophilopoulou observes that the *Code* "is the book that has had the greatest repercussions on mankind after the Bible."[15]

Foreign Wars

At the same time that Justinian was reforming the Byzantine legal code, he was also engaged in a series of wars of conquest, first against North Africa, then Italy, and finally Spain. The emperor wanted to restore the boundaries of the old Roman Empire at its height. In the end he failed to do so, although under him the Byzantine Empire reached its greatest extent.

Justinian's wars were expensive, and the emperor quickly consumed the 320,000 pounds (145,075kg) of gold that had been in the imperial treasury when he took the throne. He then had to resort to heavy and unpopular taxes to keep his armies in the field.

Paying his soldiers was one of Justinian's biggest headaches. The imperial army was made up of mercenaries from all over the empire, Europe, and the Middle East who fought for pay, not out of loyalty to lord or country or cause. It was thus difficult for Justinian to control his armies' pay rates or secure their dedication. Mercenary troops sometimes mutinied during battles, and they lost more than one fight by stopping to loot rather than pursue the enemy. Regular pay made them more manageable and less prone to impulsive looting.

General Belisarius

Byzantine soldiers were also more reliable when they had superior leadership. Justinian found such military excellence in Belisarius, the general who had so successfully crushed the Nika riot. Like Justinian, Belisarius was of peasant stock, born in what would become western Bulgaria. He was one of the greatest of the empire's many generals, winning more battles than any other Byzantine commander of his day.

Belisarius's great success had much to do with his equipping his soldiers with good weapons and armor. Each of his elite troops carried a lance, a long sword, and a bow, and each wore mail, a protective coat made up of small interlocking metal rings that was a significant improvement on earlier battle gear. From this beginning grew a uniformly equipped and trained Byzantine army that would be the most powerful military force in Europe for centuries to come.

Justinian I and the Law

One of Justinian's major goals was to reform the Byzantine legal code. In the following, found at the beginning of The Civil Law, *translated by Samuel P. Scott, the emperor instructs the head of his law commission on the committee's duties.*

"We order you to read and revise the books relating to the Roman law drawn up by the jurists of antiquity . . . so that all the substance [of these books] may be collected, and as far as may be possible, there shall remain no laws either similar to or inconsistent with one another, but that there may be compiled from them a summary which will take the place of all.

You shall divide the entire law into fifty books . . . ; and that all the ancient law which has been in a confused condition for almost fourteen hundred years shall be embraced in the said fifty books.

All legal authors shall possess equal authority, and no preference shall be given to any, because all of them are neither superior nor inferior to one another. We only desire that legal procedure to prevail which has been most frequently employed, or which long custom has established."

The Justinian court was an important part of Byzantine society. Here, a judge oversees the trial of a woman accused of adultery.

War with Persia

Before Justinian could launch this general and army into a war of conquest, he had to end a war with the Persian Empire that had broken out in 527. The two empires were ancient enemies and shared a long common border. Relations between the two states were always uneasy, and tensions periodically erupted into open warfare.

After five years of warfare, during which Belisarius won one major battle and lost another, neither side was close to a victory. Justinian became impatient to end this protracted conflict, which tied up troops that he wanted to use in his reconquest of the empire's western territories. Finally, the emperor bought peace with a promised yearly payment to Persia of 11,000 pounds (4,987kg) of gold.

Conquest of North Africa

Despite having sworn with the Persian ruler to the Everlasting Peace of 532, Justinian would find himself at war with Persia twice more, in 540 and 549. However, in 532 he could turn his attention to the former lands of the old Western Roman Empire.

In June 533 Belisarius sailed for Carthage in North Africa, which had been overrun by the German Vandals a century before. Although outnumbered, Belisarius's eighteen thousand soldiers easily defeated the Vandals in two major battles. The Vandals, who had been a fearsome menace in the fifth century, had declined militarily and were no match for the imperial troops, trained and armed by Belisarius and hardened by their recent war with Persia. North Africa was once more under the rule of an emperor.

Byzantine General Belisarius was the most successful military commander of his time.

(opposite) Byzantine General Narses was a rival of General Belisarius.

Invasion of Italy

Justinian's next target was the Ostrogothic kingdom in Italy. The Byzantine invasion began in 536 and at first went well. Belisarius quickly captured Sicily and then crossed to the mainland, moving north along the west coast of the Italian peninsula to Rome. The Ostrogoths were politically divided, and their resistance was light. The imperial army marched into Rome unopposed as the city's citizens cheered Belisarius as their liberator.

Meanwhile, the Ostrogoths drew all their forces together and surrounded Rome. Belisarius had five thousand men with which to defend the city against siege by 150,000 Goths. Despite the overwhelming odds against the Byzantines, the imperial soldiers held the city, and after a year the Goths retreated to their capital at Ravenna.

By this time Byzantine reinforcements had arrived to support Belisarius. However, three years of fighting remained before the surrender of the Goths. According to historian Robert Browning, rivalry and friction between Belisarius and another imperial general, Narses, led to an argument "in the Roman headquarters, [where] operations were launched and cancelled, and backbiting and intrigue became the order of the day."[16] This feuding ended with the destruction of an imperial garrison and much of the town of Milan in 539. Narses was recalled to Constantinople, and in the next year Belisarius took Ravenna in the course of pretending to accept the Goths' offer to become their king.

Belisarius in Italy

During Byzantine general Belisarius's 536 invasion of Italy, he found himself surrounded at Rome by a large army of Ostrogoths and wrote to Emperor Justinian I for help, as reported in Procopius's History of the Wars, *quoted in Robert Browning's* Justinian and Theodora.

"We have appointed a large part of the soldiers to garrison forts in Sicily and Italy, which we have been able to conquer, and that we have left an army of only five thousand. The enemy are coming against us to the number of one hundred and fifty thousand. . . . We were nearly buried beneath the multitude of their spears. Later, when the barbarians made an attempt on the [city] wall with their entire army and attacked it over its whole length, they came very near to taking us and the city at first blow.

If the barbarians defeat us now, we shall be driven out of your Italy and lose the army as well, and in addition shall bear the great shame of our failure. I refrain from mentioning that we should give the impression of having abandoned the citizens of Rome, who have thought less of their safety than of their loyalty to your empire. And so even our successes will turn out but the prelude to disaster."

This illustration depicts the victorious General Belisarius entering Rome after defeating the Visigoths.

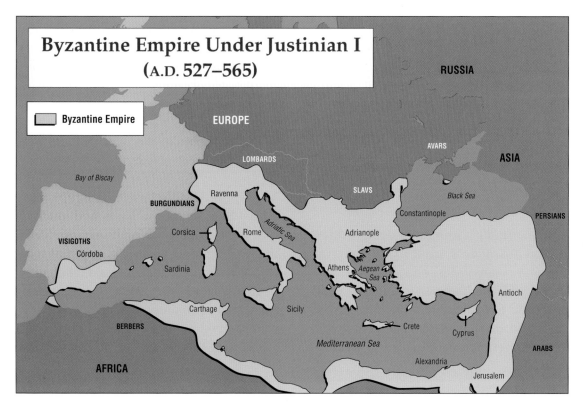

Byzantine Empire Under Justinian I (A.D. 527–565)

Byzantine Empire

RUSSIA
EUROPE
AVARS
ASIA
LOMBARDS
Bay of Biscay
SLAVS
Black Sea
Ravenna
BURGUNDIANS
Constantinople
PERSIANS
VISIGOTHS
Corsica
Rome
Adrianople
Córdoba
Adriatic Sea
Sardinia
Athens
Aegean Sea
Antioch
Carthage
Sicily
Crete
Cyprus
BERBERS
Mediterranean Sea
ARABS
AFRICA
Alexandria
Jerusalem

The Fall of Rome

Belisarius returned to Constantinople to celebrate his Italian victories. However, three years later, news came that the Ostrogoths had successfully recaptured Rome and other Italian cities. Belisarius returned immediately to Italy, where he eventually retook Rome. However, Rome was to change hands twice more, and years of fighting were to pass before the Goths were driven from Italy in 552 by Belisarius's onetime imperial rival Narses.

After over fifteen years of war, the remains of the Western Roman Empire had disintegrated. Rome itself was wrecked more thoroughly by this war than by all the previous barbarian raids combined. The westernmost provinces of the old Roman Empire, such as Gaul, remained forever outside the Byzantine Empire, which now lacked the resources to conquer them. Only southern Spain was occupied by Byzantine troops for a time beginning in 554. So the fall of Rome, which had begun in the fifth century, was completed by the middle of the sixth, and it was the heirs of Rome, the Byzantines, who played a large role in ending the old empire.

Imperial Fears

Despite the destructiveness of these Italian battles, Belisarius's military victories earned him the personal loyalty of his troops and the admiration of the citizens of Constantinople. As Procopius wrote:

> [The people] took delight in watching Belisarius as he came forth from

his home each day. . . . For his progress resembled a crowded festival procession, since he was always escorted by a large number of [Vandals and Goths]. Furthermore, he had a fine figure, and was tall and remarkably handsome. But his conduct was so meek, and his manners so affable that he seemed like a very poor man, and one of no repute.[17]

Belisarius's fame, however, undermined Justinian's trust in his general. Popular commanders had seized thrones in the past, and Justinian feared that Belisarius had the same intention. Thus, in 548 Justinian recalled Belisarius and forced him into retirement. Yet, for all of Justinian's suspicions Belisarius never gave any hint that he had designs on the emperorship. He remained loyal to Justinian and the empire until his death in 565. Justinian himself died of old age a few months later.

Under Justinian the Byzantine Empire reached its greatest extent—to the existing territory of the Balkan peninsula, Asia Minor, the Middle East, and Egypt were added Italy, southern Spain, and much of the remainder of North Africa. More important, under Justinian, imperial society took the shape that it would retain until its end. This society was highly organized, ruled by an emperor with supreme authority and obedient in all aspects of life to the Christian Church.

Chapter Three

The Byzantine Church and State

Justinian I, as emperor, was the supreme head of the Byzantine government. Also known as the *Basileus,* Greek for "King of Kings," the Byzantine ruler was the most powerful individual in the empire. His decrees automatically became law, and no one in the empire could overturn these laws. Likewise, within the Byzantine Empire the emperor was the head of the Christian Church; there was no such distinction between king and pope as there was in Europe. Consequently, political and theological issues were often one and the same, and a single decision determined both Church and state affairs.

Imperial Duties

As chief administrator of the empire, the emperor was briefed daily by secretaries and imperial officials on conditions across the Byzantine state. All government departments operated under his direct order because only the emperor had the authority to set policy. It was the emperor who, among other things, determined the amount of tax the average citizen paid, who ordered army units from one imperial post to another, and who decided how much would be spent on erecting new buildings in Byzantine cities.

In addition to his administrative duties, the emperor presided over all important festivals, holiday games, state banquets, and religious events. As one anonymous Byzantine put it, "when there is no Augusta [emperor], it is impossible to celebrate the festivals."[18]

Imperial Advisers and Bureaucrats

To aid in the performance of these duties, the emperor had a number of hand-picked advisers who formed a cabinet, which met regularly with the emperor to discuss administrative appointments, problems at home and abroad, proposed laws, and daily management of imperial affairs.

Below the imperial cabinet were many layers of officials and bureaucrats who carried out the emperor's orders. The most important official was the *magister officiorum*, or "master of offices," who appointed the thousands of bureaucrats staffing the various governmental departments. In addition to this duty the master of offices was in charge of foreign relations, the postal system, and the emperor's bodyguard. He was also the empire's spymaster, running a string of informers who enabled him to monitor potentially dangerous and ambitious subordinates.

In addition to these officials the emperor also had the aid of the Byzantine senate, which was modeled on that of Rome. Senators were male aristocrats appointed by the emperor; their office and title were hereditary. The senate drew up legislation and presented it to the emperor for his approval or rejection: The senate had no power to pass laws on its own.

Imperial Electors

The senate did exercise power in one matter: the choosing of an imperial heir. The emperorship was not hereditary. Instead, each emperor selected his own heir, who might be a son, some other relative, or even a close and trusted friend or adviser. The emperor's choice, however, did not automatically become the imperial heir. The candidate could only be crowned after having been formally elected by three bodies known as electors: the senate, the army, and the citizens of Constantinople. These electors also had the authority to remove an incompetent or disliked emperor; in fact, any one of the three electors had the power to order his removal, even without the consent of the other two.

The Power of the Army

Of the three elector groups the army was the most important. Emperors who wished to see their successor approved or to remain in office had to win the support of imperial soldiers. A Byzantine ruler could ignore the senate and the people of Constantinople, but to ignore the army courted disaster. Angry soldiers often refused to carry out imperial orders, an act that could leave the empire open to attack. As historian Steven Runciman points out, "the empire was beset with enemies; never for a moment could the Government feel free from the danger of foreign invasion."[19]

Angry soldiers also threatened the emperor with open revolt, which occurred periodically over the centuries and resulted in several emperors' execution, imprisonment, or exile. Other emperors were blinded, an act that made them ineligible to hold the throne.

Funding the Empire

Regular pay for army troops was generally the best way of insuring their loyalty. The military, however, was only one of the necessary expenses in running the Byzantine government. The imperial treasury also had to cover the salaries of imperial bureaucrats and the cost of constructing and maintaining public buildings.

Fortunately, despite the occasional economic crisis, the Byzantine Empire's finances were sound because, with Constantinople the major trade center between Europe and Asia, it was rich. Durant writes

Imperial Ceremony

One of the Byzantine emperor's major duties was taking part in the many Byzantine festivals, banquets, religious events, and other state occasions. The following account by Liudprand of Cremona, found in his collected works, describes one such ceremony that took place just before Palm Sunday.

"The emperor makes a payment in gold coins to [the] officers of the court, each one receiving a sum proportionate to his office. . . . The first to be summoned was the marshal of the palace, who carried off his money, not in his hands but on his shoulders, together with four cloaks of honor. After him came the commander in chief of the army and the lord high admiral of the fleet. These being of equal rank received an equal number of money bags and cloaks, which they did not carry off on their shoulders but with some assistance dragged laboriously away. After them came twenty-four [administrators], who each received twenty-four pounds [11kg] of gold coins together with two new cloaks, [and] after them came a huge crowd of minor dignitaries. . . . This was [not] all done in one day. It began on the fifth day of the week at six o'clock in the morning and went on till ten, and the emperor finished his part in the proceedings on the sixth and seventh day."

Emperor Theophilos reads an imperial decree. Presiding over formal ceremonies was an important part of a Byzantine emperor's duties.

that "from the fifth century to the fifteenth Constantinople remained the greatest market and shipping center in the world," for ancient "Roman roads and bridges were kept in repair, and the creative lust for gain built maritime fleets that bound the capital with a hundred ports in East and West."[20] The imperial economy was so strong that the *nomisma*, the Byzantine gold piece, was the standard coin through-

---

A Visit with the Emperor

Foreign visitors to the Byzantine Empire were generally impressed by much of what they saw, particularly since the Byzantines had more advanced technical skills than most of their European counterparts. The following account by the tenth-century Liuprand of Cremona in northern Italy, excerpted from his collected works, describes the author's visit to the imperial court.

"Before the emperor's seat stood a tree, made of bronze gilded over, whose branches were filled with birds, also made of gilded bronze, which uttered different cries, each according to its varying species. The throne itself was . . . of immense size and was guarded by lions, made either of bronze or of wood covered over with gold, who beat the ground with their tails and gave a dreadful roar with open mouth and quivering tongue. The emperor personally invited me to dinner with him. . . . Everything is served

in vessels, not of silver, but of gold. After the solid food, fruit is brought on in three golden bowls, which are too heavy for men to lift and come in on carriers covered over with purple cloth. Two of them are put on the table in the following way. Through openings in the ceiling hang three ropes covered with gilded leather and furnished with golden rings. These rings are attached to the handles [of] the bowls, and with four or five men helping from below, they are swung on to the table."

The lavish banquets hosted by Byzantine emperors impressed foreign visitors.

The gold coins minted by the Byzantine Empire served as the standard currency of the Mediterranean for centuries.

out the entire Mediterranean region for over eight hundred years.

The Byzantine treasury profited directly from trade monopolies in silk, purple dye, and gold embroidery, all important trade goods that were used for the ceremonial clothing of civil and religious leaders all over Europe, the Middle East, and North Africa. Indirectly, the empire made money on trade by taxing the import and export of merchandise.

Trade was not the only source of imperial revenue. The Byzantine government also taxed property and inheritance. Its revenues were further well supplied by successful state-controlled businesses and industries such as farms, cattle ranches, marble quarries, and gold and silver mines.

The Church

Much of the Byzantines' wealth was funneled into the coffers of the Church as well as the imperial treasury. Indeed, for the Byzantines there actually was no difference between Church and state, which formed essentially a single entity. In this spirit, the emperor was the head of the Church as he was the head of the state. He was the ambassador of God on Earth, and when he rode out to war, he went as God's champion and the defender of Christianity.

The emperor seldom concerned himself with day-to-day religious administration, confining his Church activities to those required by law, custom, and ceremony, such as the calling of Church councils and the appointment of Church officials. He left Church administrative duties largely to the highest-ranking Byzantine bishop, the patriarch of Constantinople. The patriarch served at the pleasure of the emper-

or, and a patriarch who angered the Byzantine ruler would soon find himself deposed and in exile. Thus, the emperor could truly say that "this man is appointed Patriarch of Constantinople . . . by our Imperial Authority"[21] as well as by the grace of God.

Religion and the Byzantines

The unification of Church and state in the person of the emperor was acknowledgment that the Church dictated every aspect of Byzantine life. According to Brinton:

Church and state were unified in the Byzantine Empire. This 14th century mosaic depicts the Virgin Mary and the baby Jesus flanked by an emperor and empress.

At every important moment in the life of every person, the Church played an important role, governing marriage, and family relations, filling leisure time, helping to determine any critical decision. Religion pervaded intellectual life: The most serious intellectual problems of the age were those of theology, and they were attacked with zest by brains second to none in power. . . . Religion pervaded economic life: Business was carried on under the auspices of the Church.[22]

All Byzantine citizens—from laborers to merchants to aristocrats—took part in religious debates about such subjects as how exactly God, Christ, and the Holy Spirit were related to each other and whether Satan or God was more powerful on Earth. They argued religion during work breaks, in shops, at mealtimes, in taverns, or in any other place where two or more Byzantines stopped to talk.

The Monastic Life

Reflecting their religious enthusiasm, Byzantines held members of the clergy—priests, bishops, and monks—in high regard. Above all others, however, imperial citizens respected the monks, who were members of religious retreats, or monasteries. Monks gave up all possessions, including property, money, and personal clothing, and devoted themselves to prayer, meditation, and religious study. As part of the clergy, many monks served as chaplains to the largest Byzantine churches, which were often attached to monasteries.

Monks held their special place in Byzantine society because the quiet meditation of the monastery appealed to many Byzantines. Runciman observes that "the Byzantines most admired those who gave up the pleasures of the world and prepared themselves for eternity by contemplation."[23]

The Bishop of Rome

The Byzantine emperor claimed authority over the monasteries and all other organs of the Church not only within the borders of his empire but also in Western Europe and indeed over all Christians everywhere. This claim challenged the still-powerful bishops of the western church.

The most important bishop in the western regions was that of Rome—the pope. The pope's authority came in large part from his being in Rome, which remained as a center of power and Christianity even long after the Western Roman Empire collapsed. Rome had been the city from which most civil court decisions had come, and the bishop of Rome retained the power to decide crucial religious matters. Additionally, the ruling of an early Church council gave Rome authority over Constantinople because the Italian city was the older of the two. Finally, the pope's authority rested on Christians' belief that he inherited his post from St. Peter, traditionally considered the most important of Christ's disciples and the first bishop of Rome. The pope claimed divine authority, therefore, by occupying St. Peter's position.

Friction existed between the Roman pope and the Byzantine emperor because the pope refused to acknowledge the emperor as head of the Church. As far as

Monks, who lived in monasteries such as this one in Greece, were held in high regard by Byzantine citizens.

Rome was concerned, no civil leader could outrank the Church's spiritual head.

Doctrine and Heresy

Rome was not the only important Christian center with whom Constantinople had uneasy relations. Both Alexandria in Egypt and Antioch in Syria had patriarchs who ranked just after that of Constantinople. A good deal of political rivalry existed between the three Byzantine cities because all were about equal in size and wealth. However, all the political power resided in Constantinople. These political jealousies spilled over into Church affairs, with the patriarchs of all three cities jockeying for power within the Church.

Much of this power struggle revolved around determining Church doctrine, or beliefs. It was not always clear which doctrines the Church should support since many interpretations existed as to what

Christ had taught. Even Christ's relationship to God was open to question. For example, the fourth-century priest Arius of Alexandria proposed that God was superior to Christ because God had fathered Jesus. The opposing view was that God and Christ, along with the Holy Spirit, were equal parts of a single mystical entity known as the Trinity.

The Church generally dealt with opposing doctrines by calling a council of bishops who would listen to the arguments of all

The Council of Ephesus

The following letter is quoted in Creeds, Councils, and Controversies, *edited by James Stevenson. In it Flavian, the patriarch of Constantinople, complains to Pope Leo I of his treatment by Dioscurus, the patriarch of Alexandria, at the 449 Council of Ephesus. Dioscurus forced the council to endorse Monophysitism, which Flavian sees as a disaster for the Church.*

"Everything is in complete confusion: the laws of the Church are abolished: in matters of faith all is lost: pious souls are bewildered by controversy. Men do not speak of the faith of the Fathers, but the fact is that [Monophysitism is] now preached and praised by Dioscurus, bishop of Alexandria, and those who think as he does. For his decree is the confirmation of this 'faith,' as is the vote of those bishops who had been compelled by force to agree to it.

[Dioscurus gave] orders that I and the bishops who sat in judgment with me . . . should not be allowed any hearing or the utterance of a word of defense on any point; threatening also some with imprisonment, others with various punishments, he clears the way for an immediate reading of an account of the matter previously prepared."

Pope Leo I, pictured here, opposed Monophysitism, the heretical belief that Christ's nature was completely divine.

concerned and then decide which position to support. In the case of Arius and his so-called Arian controversy, the council sided with his opponents. Those beliefs, such as Arius's, that were finally rejected by the Church were condemned as heresies, and their followers were subject to bitter and often violent persecution.

Monophysitism

Constantinople found itself in a bitter struggle with Alexandria in the fifth century over one such heresy, Monophysitism. Monophysitism also dealt with the nature of Christ. One school of Christian thought proposed that, since Jesus had been born a man, he was human, but since he was also a part of God, he was also divine. Thus, the conclusion was that Christ's nature was an equal mixture of divine and human.

The Monophysites, on the other hand, claimed that Christ's nature was completely divine. They argued that the part of

Christ that was human no longer existed because it had been swallowed up and absorbed by the divine.

Alexandria was the center of Monophysitism, while Constantinople and Rome held to the opposing view. Flavian, the patriarch of Constantinople, and Pope Leo I agreed to an alliance to fight Monophysitism. Christophilopoulou notes that the two churchmen "looked with an unfavorable eye on the growing power and ambitious designs of the patriarchal throne of Alexandria, and found it a convenient opportunity to assist in the humiliation of a troublesome rival."[24] However, humiliating Dioscurus, the patriarch of Alexandria and up to this point next in authority to the bishop of Rome, proved difficult.

In 449 a Church council convened at Ephesus in Asia Minor to decide the Monophysitism issue. At the council Patriarch Dioscurus arrived with a large party of Alexandrian clergy. Among Dioscurus's followers was a group of well-armed priests who physically threatened and intimidated the other attendees into endorsing Monophysitism.

The Alexandrians' tactics led to a storm of protest and a labeling of the meeting as the Robber Council. As a result of the protests, the Ephesus council's decision was not accepted, and a new council was held in 451 at Chalcedon, a city located across the Bosporous from Constantinople. At Constantinople's urging the Council of Chalcedon rejected Monophysitism, declaring it a heresy. It also removed the Patriarch Dioscurus from office and gave the patriarch of Constantinople higher authority than that of Alexandria. Thus began a split in the Church between the Egyptian and the Greek factions that involved ongoing ecclesiastical conflict throughout the Byzantine era.

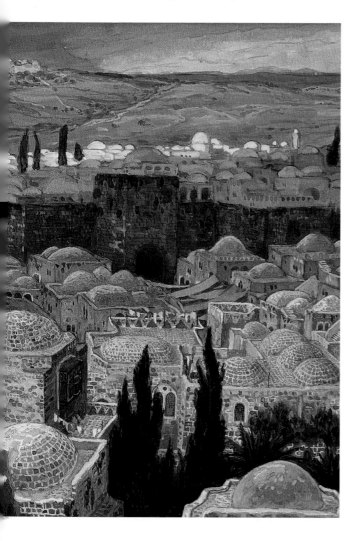

This painting depicts the pagan temple that Roman Emperor Hadrian built in Jerusalem. Constantine replaced it with the Shrine of the Holy Sepulchre .

Heretics and Pagans

All factions of the Byzantine Church sought to destroy heresy, and their primary weapon was Byzantine civil law: At first heretics faced heavy fines and loss of their property; later, emperors passed harsher laws that relied on torture and execution to punish and eliminate heresy.

Similar laws were also aimed at destroying any pagan, or non-Christian, religions practiced in the empire. The major targets for these laws were the old Greek and Roman religions, which were based on the worship of many gods and animist spirits in nature. Pagans were forbidden to worship, and they were fined if caught doing so. Their temples were torn down or convened to other uses. Known pagans risked their lives by going out in public where they might be attacked and killed by anti-pagan mobs.

Restrictions were also placed on Jews. Although Jews were allowed to worship, they had to pay for the privilege with such high taxes that many were forced to sell their children into slavery. Imperial law demanded the death penalty for any Jew who married a Christian. Like heretics and pagans, Jews were the target of rampaging mobs, who killed any Jew they found and burned down synagogues.

Religion and Revolt

Such persecution destroyed the classical pagan religion, which was already in decline even before Christianity became the state religion of the Roman Empire. However, persecution was not effective against the Jews or the Christian heretics, both of whom clung to their beliefs.

Some heresies even flourished under the empire's oppressive laws, Monophysitism in particular. Even after the Council of Chalcedon the citizens of Alexandria refused to give up Monophysitism, which came to symbolize their resistance to the central imperial authority. Antioch, the other great rival of Constantinople, also embraced Monophysitism. Ostrogorsky writes:

> The conflict between the . . . Church of Constantinople and the monophysite Churches of the Christian East became the burning problem in ecclesiastical [religious] and secular [nonreligious] politics of the early Byzantine Empire. Monophysitism served as an outlet for the political separatist tendencies of Egypt and Syria; it was the rallying cry of [those in] opposition to Byzantine rule.[25]

Religious persecution was the darker side of Byzantine Christianity. A more positive and ultimately more lasting manifestation was the fusing of Christian artistic and literary traditions with those of the old classical culture to create the unique art, architecture, and writings of the Byzantine Empire.

Chapter Four

The Flowering of Byzantine Culture

The culture of the Byzantine Empire during the reign of Justinian I—and for centuries afterward—was the most advanced in Europe. Until the twelfth century European societies in general were too fragmented and politically unstable to be able to support schools in any large numbers. Likewise, these societies' artistic and literary efforts were limited as warfare and basic survival consumed people's energies. The Byzantines, on the other hand, had a strong, wealthy state to which thousands of teachers, artists, writers, and theologians contributed their literary and artistic talents.

Cultural Roots

Many factors affected the development of Byzantine culture: One important element was the empire's well-recognized classical legacy. The Byzantines continued to read and treasure ancient Greek and Roman literature and philosophy, even as most ancient Greek and Latin texts were

lost in western Europe. Thus, the works of Aristotle, Plato, Sophocles, and many others were not only preserved in Byzantine libraries but also served as guides for Byzantine thinking, writing, and teaching.

This classical past occasionally collided with another component of Byzantine culture, Christianity. Indeed, the Church tried at times to eliminate the Greek and Roman features of Byzantine civilization. With rare exceptions the clergy did not approve of the old classical works, which they viewed as anti-Christian. However, despite the Church's increasing role in Byzantine education, it failed completely to stamp out the empire's non-Christian heritage.

From the East

In addition to these classical and Christian influences, Byzantine culture was also affected by the empire's contact with various Middle Eastern societies, such as that of the Persian Empire. Middle Eastern culture tended to be more ornate, refined, and

The Byzantines favored elaborately decorated silk coats over plain Roman togas.

ritualistic than that of the more matter-of-fact Romans. For example, from Persia the Byzantines borrowed a complex of rituals surrounding the emperor. Brinton observes: "Silence in his presence was the rule. He spoke and gave his commands through simple, brief, and established formulas. When he gave gifts, his subjects had their hands beneath their cloaks, a Persian ritual gesture implying that the touch of a mere human hand would soil his. . . . On public occasions the emperor was acclaimed in song, to the sound of silver trumpets."[26] Like that of the Persians, Byzantine imperial etiquette was so complicated that entire books were written on the subject.

The Byzantines further replaced undecorated Roman togas with eastern silk coats sporting intricate designs. The Middle East preferred, as Durant notes, "rich ornament to stern simplicity, gorgeous silks to shapeless togas."[27]

Education

Despite this strong Middle Eastern influence, it was the Byzantines' Greek and Roman past that instilled in them a deep love and respect for learning. Education was highly valued, and its lack was viewed as a serious handicap.

Just what proportion of the Byzantine population was formally educated is unknown. Certainly, the number of Byzantines who could read and write was much higher than in western Europe, where almost no one was literate, including the aristocracy. In the Byzantine Empire most upper- and middle-class men and women were literate, as were some of the working class.

Schooling

For those who did receive an education, learning generally began at home, where mothers instructed their children in the basics of writing and proper speech. Then, at around age six, in all the cities and towns—and even in some small villages—the children entered state-run schools, which were available to the offspring of any free citizen. Here, children received further training in writing and began studying other subjects. Historian Tamara Talbot Rice explains:

> Children were first instructed in grammar—a term which included reading and writing. This was followed by more advanced grammar, syntax, and introduction to the classics; each pupil was expected to learn 50 lines of Homer by heart each day.

Education was highly valued in the Byzantine Empire. These sixth-century tablets were part of a book containing math exercises.

. . . At the age of 14 their time was spent in studying rhetoric [the effective use of language]: this included pronunciation and enunciation as well as the study of great prose writers such as Demosthenes. In their last year at school students were taught philosophy, the sciences, and the "four arts"—arithmetic, geometry, music, and astronomy.[28]

In the program Rice describes, however, these subjects were not taught as the ancient Greeks and Romans taught them before the rise of Christianity. The influence of the Church extended to redefining and reinterpreting truth and knowledge in light of Christian beliefs. For example, it was not unusual for school texts to omit references to Roman gods and goddesses and to insert sections detailing Christian virtues and the teachings of Christ. Thus, schools were a primary source of religious training. Above all else, school-attending children were expected to know the Bible by heart.

Late in adolescence, some students moved on to higher education, such as was offered at the imperial university at Constantinople. According to Nicholas, "although formal higher education was normally restricted to men, many aristocratic women studied under tutors."[29] The curricula for both university and tutored students essentially consisted of advanced study of the same subjects offered to younger students.

Teachers

The Byzantine educational system depended on excellent teachers, whom the Byzantines set out to attract and hold to high standards. All instructors had to pass state examinations and possess a teaching license. Further, to encourage capable people to become teachers, salaries were high, being paid by either the imperial or local government.

Such practices ensured that gifted and educated men and women became teachers. Among the most famous Byzantine teachers was the fifth-century philosopher and mathematician Hypatia, a follower of the ancient Greek philosopher Plato. Hypatia's contemporary, the Byzantine historian Socrates (not to be confused with the great ancient Greek philosopher of the same name), wrote of her that she "far surpassed the other philosophers of her time."[30] She taught a variety of subjects, such as astronomy, solid geometry, and arithmetic. Hypatia's fame was such that her students came from all over the empire to study with her.

Cultural Limitations

Despite its many merits and excellent teachers, Byzantine education was not innovative: Its focus was the classical past and the Christian present. This dependence put strict limits on original thinking, and during their thousand-year history the Byzantines produced little that was original in philosophy, mathematics, or science.

Their literature was almost as limited. As original writers, the Byzantines were noteworthy mostly for histories and religious works. Literary works of other sorts were rare and of little importance.

Histories such as those of the sixth-century writer Procopius were immensely popular. Runciman observes:

The Life of a Saint

Books about the lives of saints and other holy people were very popular among Byzantine readers. The following excerpt, translated by Elizabeth Dawes and Norman H. Baynes, is from their book Three Byzantine Saints. *It is from an account of the life of the seventh-century saint Theodore of Sykeon, who here becomes the target of the evil sorcerer Theodotus, who sees the saint as his mortal enemy.*

[Theodotus] sent his envoys to attack the Saint and, if possible, so to injure him that he should die. Those who were sent did not dare even to show themselves to [St. Theodore] face to face whilst he was awake but waited for his hour of sleeping; and then stealthily, like thieves, they sought to attack him—thieves indeed they were and powerless to harm him openly. But the divine power which guarded him routed them; however, the bolder in wickedness among them had the effrontery once more to draw near to him to wreak their wickedness and again the grace of God like a fire issuing from him scorched them and drove them away.

[Theodotus] became yet more infuriated, [and] inserted a deadly poison into a fish and charged some other agents of his to see to it that the Saint should eat the fish. But when the Saint through the Grace of God and through the blessing he said over the fish did not take any harm, then indeed Theodotus was ashamed at the failure of his murderous designs and [recognizing God's power] went and threw himself at the Saint's feet, wailing and weeping and begging to obtain mercy.

Elaborately decorated religious books were highly prized in the Byzantine Empire.

To judge from the number of historians and still more of popular chroniclers and the frequent editions of the chronicles, it [history] was a matter of widespread interest. The Byzantines loved to read of the past glories of the Empire; and the best-liked of the chronicles even stretched back to the Creation and Adam and Eve, and included the Tale of Troy. Past Emperors and past saints were vivid before their eyes.[31]

Religious Writings

Religious works, both books and hymns, were even more popular and successful than histories. Complex theological works produced by such famous writers as Leontius of Byzantium and Maximus the Confessor appealed to the better-educated Byzantines. On one level, these works plunged their readers deep into the mysteries of Christian faith and doctrine. On another, they were position papers defending or criticizing the many stances taken by various theologians in the endless debates over religious issues.

Even well-educated readers lost their way in these dense works of religious theory; the average citizen found such writings completely unapproachable and boring. Consequently, many literate Byzantines sought out writings that were more accessible and lively, especially works about the lives of saints and holy hermits. Saints' lives were inspirational pieces about the trials that holy men and women endured for their faith. These works described hardship, peril, and suffering and always ended with the final victory of virtue and holiness. Many of these stories were openly labeled as fiction, but they were just as popular as the stories presented as fact.

Also popular were stories about holy hermits, or anchorites. To strengthen and prove their faith, anchorites put themselves through all sorts of deprivation and physical abuse. Some went without sleep for a week or more, others ate only once a week, and still others carried heavy weights day and night. Self-inflicted wounds and whippings were common. A few, known as stylites, climbed to the top of 60-foot-high (18.3m) columns and remained standing there for the rest of their lives. The chronicles of anchorites and stylites were considered almost as inspiring as the tales of the saints and were endlessly fascinating to most Byzantine readers.

Glorious Architecture

Cramped though it was in literature, Byzantine creativity blossomed in the fine arts, which blended the Greek, Roman, Middle Eastern, and Christian elements that made up Byzantine culture and which created unique works of historic beauty. Of all the Byzantine arts architecture was the greatest, with an original Byzantine style emerging as early as the reign of Justinian I.

After the Nika riot in 532 whole sections of Constantinople were left in fire-blackened ruins. Justinian soon launched a massive rebuilding program. However, the emperor did not want just copies of the destroyed buildings; he wanted something new. Out of this imperial desire came building designs that were influenced by Roman and Middle Eastern style but that were distinctly Byzantine.

The Church of Santa Sophia

Justinian's chief architects were Anthemius of Tralles and Isidorus of Miletos, whose most famous project was the Church of Santa Sophia. The architects combined the Roman basilica, a building shaped like a cross, with the dome popular in the Middle East. According to de Camp:

> The central part covered an area 120 feet [36.6m] square. At each corner of this square rose a huge 100-foot stone pier [30.5m]. These piers in turn supported four arches, each 60 feet [18.3m] high. The arches upheld a dome . . . , flattened at the top. On the east and west sides of the square, half-domes supported by semicircular walls buttressed the structure and provided room for the chancel and nave. The inside was partitioned by arcades mounted on rows of columns. . . . Most of the ornate decoration was inside in the form of gilding, mosaics, and colored marble; the outside was left functionally bare.[32]

Ten thousand workers labored over five years to build Santa Sophia, and the result awed worldly Byzantines as well as foreign visitors to Constantinople. The Byzantine writer Procopius wrote that "one feels at once that it is the work not of man's effort or industry, but in truth the work of the divine power; and the spirit, mount-ing to heaven, realizes that here God is very near."[33]

Anthemius and Isidorus built well, for Santa Sophia still stands today, having survived fifteen hundred years of earthquakes, war, riots, and fires. The domed roof they introduced with Santa Sophia became the major feature of all Byzantine public buildings, and the dome plus basilica became the standard design of all Byzantine churches. It was quickly copied not only in the East but also in western Europe.

Mosaics and Paintings

For the most part the exteriors of Byzantine public buildings and churches were rather plain and bare of decoration. However, the interiors were extremely elaborate. The floors and walls were often covered with mosaics, another of the great imperial arts. These mosaics were patterns and pictures made up of thousands of marble or glass cubes in a vast array of brilliant colors, notably gold. Marble was used predominantly for floors and glass for the walls.

The glass cubes, some of them backed with gold leaf, ranged from the size of a pinhead to 1 inch (2.54cm) across. The smallest pieces were used for fine detail work such as a figure's eyes and the largest for broad fields such as a scene's background. Byzantine artists hand set each cube, one at a time, into a layer of damp plaster spread across the surface; the mosaic was permanently set as the plaster dried.

Over time, wall mosaics gave way to wall paintings, with Byzantine subject matter remaining mostly religious. Naturally,

Byzantine Art and Architecture

(Above) exterior of the **Santa Sophia** in Istanbul.

(Below) a Byzantine ivory diptich of Christ and the Virgin Mary.

(Above) interior of the **Santa Sophia** in Istanbul.

(Below) fresco in the monastery of Variaam, Greece.

(Above) mosaic at Basilica of San Marco.

(Right) Byzantine jewelry was fashioned of gold and precious stones.

(Below) Byzantine mosaic map of the Holy Land.

pictures in churches depicted religious scenes but so did art in government and other civic and private buildings. Mosaics and paintings particularly represented Christ, the Virgin Mary, or one of the many Byzantine saints.

Byzantine religious art, like architecture, shows multicultural influences. The figures and backgrounds are always two-dimensional; that is, they appear flat and without depth, in the tradition of Middle Eastern art. Figures are also presented in certain standard poses, and their facial features are distorted, with very large eyes, much like those found in ancient Egyptian portraits. The figures are in robes and the backgrounds are covered in drapes, techniques copied from the ancient Greeks that indicate that the subjects are indoors.

Besides mosaics and wall paintings, other art forms flourished in the Byzantine Empire. Among these were gold and silver working, ivory carving, and weaving. Sculpture, however, was not popular. Although favored by many emperors, who had statues made of themselves, Byzantine Christianity discouraged religious statues as idol worship.

The Byzantines would maintain their cultural superiority over other Europeans for many centuries to come. During much of the Middle Ages Europeans from outside the empire visited Constantinople and marveled at Byzantine architecture and art. They often came to study in Byzantine schools and to explore the contents of imperial libraries. Yet within a few years of the death of Justinian I the empire experienced a crisis that put the survival of schools or arts or political structure in doubt.

Chapter Five

Threats from Without: The Armies of Persia and Islam

Upon the death of the Emperor Justinian I in 565, the Byzantine Empire was the largest and most powerful state in Europe. It was rich in culture and in trade profits, yet within fifty years it would teeter on the brink of disaster, much of its land threatened by one invader after another.

Justinian's Legacy

The empire's troubles arose directly out of Justinian's reign. First, Justinian had left the empire in deep financial trouble. During his thirty-eight-year rule the Byzantines were almost always at war. As a consequence, the treasury was depleted in part by the huge sums needed to pay for mercenary armies and military supplies.

On top of the war expenses were the costs of Justinian's ambitious rebuilding of Constantinople after the 532 Nika revolt. The Church of Santa Sophia alone cost 320,000 pounds (145,100kg) of gold,

which was the content of the imperial treasury when Justinian came to power. And Santa Sophia was only one of dozens of buildings the emperor sponsored.

At Justinian's death the Byzantine government was close to broke. The next three emperors—Justin II, Tiberius II, and Maurice—barely kept the empire afloat by heavily taxing Byzantine citizens.

Second, Justinian had left the empire with a military crisis. The Byzantine army was scattered all over the newly expanded empire. Many units were tied up fighting in Africa against fierce nomads called Berbers, and in Italy, against a German tribe, the Lombards, who had successfully taken much of northern Italy from the imperial troops. The remainder of the army formed a thin line of defense that was not strong enough to protect the empire's borders. The Byzantine state was open to attack, and that attack was not long in coming.

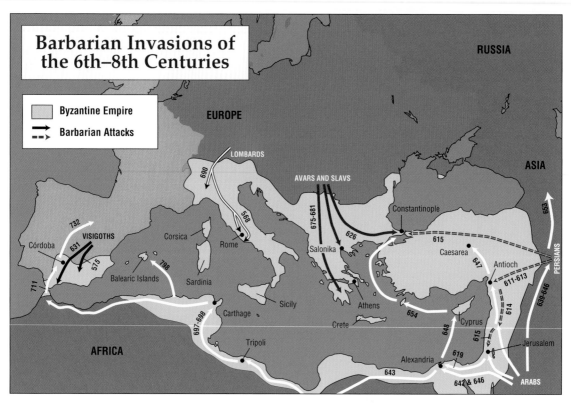

The Slavs and the Avars

To the north of Constantinople the Byzantine Empire's Balkan territory was being raided by a new group of barbarians, the Slavs. To stop these raids, the Byzantines arranged with the Avars, a people related to the Huns, to attack the Slavs. The empire hoped that this attack would keep the Slavs too busy fighting the Avars to have time for raiding the Balkans.

The plan misfired badly, as large groups of Slavs, fleeing the Avars, drove deep into the Balkans, their warriors occasionally threatening Constantinople itself. Many of the Slavs ended up staying and occupying the Balkan peninsula. Further, in 582 the Avars turned on the Byzantines and began attacking the

Balkans with armies composed of conquered Slavs.

Rebels and Persians

Over the next two decades the imperial government did its best to stop the Avars. However, Emperor Maurice received little support from the imperial citizenry. Thousands of Byzantines fled to monasteries to escape military service. In 602 Maurice ordered the monasteries to close their doors to new members until the threat posed by the Avars was over. The emperor's action enraged the monks, who with the aid of the Blues and Greens, prodded the people into revolt.

Ostrogorsky writes that while the rebels rioted in Constantinople, the army fighting the Avars mutinied, "being worn out and dispirited at the prospect of a war whose end was not in sight."[34] After killing their senior officers and choosing a junior officer, Phocas, as their new leader, the army marched on the capital and joined forces with the Blues and the Greens. Maurice and his family were killed, and Phocas became the new emperor.

To the east the Persians took advantage of the confusion caused by the Byzantine revolution and hit the empire hard, driving deep into imperial territory. Taking almost all available army units, Phocas counterattacked, but was unable to stop the Persians, who seized and occupied large chunks of the Byzantine state, including Syria and Egypt. Meanwhile, in his unsuccessful campaign against his eastern enemy, the emperor had stripped away so many troops from the Balkans that the Avars marched far into Byzantine territory, even capturing farmland near Constantinople. The Byzantine Empire appeared doomed.

A New Emperor

In 610, when Byzantine fortunes were at their lowest, Heraclius, son of the military commander of Africa, killed Phocas and seized the imperial throne. It took the new emperor ten hard years to renew, as Durant notes, "the morale of the people, the strength of the army, and the resources of the treasury."[35]

One of Heraclius's first actions was to rebuild the army. In the provinces of Asia Minor he established military districts called themes. Each theme's commander was also the area's civilian governor, and its soldiers settled and farmed the province. Each army theme was composed of between 3,000 and 4,000 soldiers; eventually, with the establishment of more themes the Byzantine emperors assembled a provincial army of 120,000 men.

The theme system made for a far better and far more reliable army since the empire no longer had to depend upon expensive and untrustworthy mercenaries. Brinton writes, "In each theme the troops were recruited from the native population; in return for their services, the sturdy, independent yeoman farmers were granted land but they were not allowed to dispose of it or to evade their duties as soldiers. Their sons inherited the property along with the obligation to fight. . . . From the start, one of the themes was naval."[36]

In addition to the troops of the themes, the emperor also maintained army and navy units under his own control at Constantinople.

A New Military Organization

The Byzantine themes were organized in combination with other units into several regiments, both infantry and cavalry, each commanded by a general. Junior officers and noncommissioned officers led smaller units of various size within each regiment. Supporting the regiments were a medical corps, an intelligence corps, and a signal corps that used mirrors to flash messages back and forth from one position to another.

The Byzantine navy was much smaller than the army, with only a single admiral. The naval forces commanded by this admiral were divided into small fleets of warships, each vessel carrying one hundred to three hundred sailors. The ships were propelled by both sails and oars and had battering rams with which to sink enemy vessels.

Winning Back the Empire

In the spring of 622 Heraclius set out to push the Persians back beyond the empire's eastern border. He went first to the themes of Asia Minor to collect and train the soldiers there over the summer. Heraclius, according to Ostrogorsky, "had concentrated on the study of military science." Under this emperor, "the use of cavalry in the Byzantine army became increasingly important," with Heraclius attaching "special significance to the lightly armed mounted archers."[37]

In the autumn the campaign against Persia began. It was a long, difficult war, and at one point in 626 the Avars laid siege to Constantinople, while the Persians threatened the city from across the Bosporus. The imperial army first routed the Avars and then the Persians.

After their defeat at Constantinople the Avars were no longer a threat to the empire. Within two years neither were the Persians. A combination of a Byzantine victory over the Persians in 627 that practically wiped out the enemy army and the overthrow of the Persian ruler a year later ended the war in 629.

War with the Arabs

Heraclius had regained all the territory lost to the Persians, and with war payments from them and contributions from the wealthy Byzantine Church, he had begun to refill the imperial treasury. The empire's prospects for safety and stability seemed good. Then in 634, only five years after the Persian victory, a new enemy struck. Arab armies under the banner of the new religion Islam stormed into Syria.

Islam, one of the world's great religions, had been founded by its prophet Muhammad in Mecca in 622. The faith quickly attracted adherents and, establishing a philosophy of military expansion, or jihad (holy war), quickly became a major force in the medieval world. Its followers, known as Muslims (Arabic for "those who submit"), had recently conquered all of Arabia, and now Islamic armies turned against the Byzantine and Persian Empires.

The Byzantine Empire, the first European state to feel the impact of the Islamic jihad, suffered numerous losses. Syria and Palestine, along with Jerusalem, fell within three years. In 641, the year Heraclius died, the Arabs took Egypt, and with that Muslim victory all of the territories regained from Persia were once more lost—this time permanently. The Byzantines suffered a final loss when North Africa was overrun by Muslim armies in 698. Thus, by the end of the seventh century almost all of the empire's land outside of western and central Asia Minor, the Balkans, and Italy was gone. As for Persia, the Byzantines' great enemy, it fell to Arab armies in 641.

The Keys to Muslim Victory

There were two key factors in the seventh-century jihad's success. First, Heraclius's defeat of Persia had been costly. Both the Byzantines and the Persians were drained by their years of war, and they were easy marks for the Muslim armies that burst out of Arabia in 634.

Second, when Heraclius regained Egypt and Syria from the Persians, he had cracked down on the Jews and the Monophysites, the latter making up the bulk of the population of these imperial provinces. Consequently, these persecuted groups saw the arrival of the Arabs as a way of

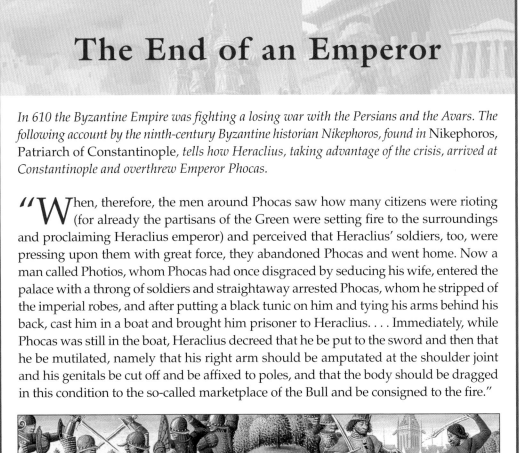

The End of an Emperor

In 610 the Byzantine Empire was fighting a losing war with the Persians and the Avars. The following account by the ninth-century Byzantine historian Nikephoros, found in Nikephoros, Patriarch of Constantinople, *tells how Heraclius, taking advantage of the crisis, arrived at Constantinople and overthrew Emperor Phocas.*

"When, therefore, the men around Phocas saw how many citizens were rioting (for already the partisans of the Green were setting fire to the surroundings and proclaiming Heraclius emperor) and perceived that Heraclius' soldiers, too, were pressing upon them with great force, they abandoned Phocas and went home. Now a man called Photios, whom Phocas had once disgraced by seducing his wife, entered the palace with a throng of soldiers and straightaway arrested Phocas, whom he stripped of the imperial robes, and after putting a black tunic on him and tying his arms behind his back, cast him in a boat and brought him prisoner to Heraclius. . . . Immediately, while Phocas was still in the boat, Heraclius decreed that he be put to the sword and then that he be mutilated, namely that his right arm should be amputated at the shoulder joint and his genitals be cut off and be affixed to poles, and that the body should be dragged in this condition to the so-called marketplace of the Bull and be consigned to the fire."

This illustration depicts the overthrow of Emperor Phocas by Heraclius in A.D. 610.

escaping imperial harassment because the Arabs did not persecute either Christians or Jews. What mattered to the Muslim Arabs was that both Christians and Jews believed as Muslims do in a single God and that they were "peoples of the Book," the holy scriptures that contributed to the Christian Bible, the Jewish Torah, and the Islamic Koran.

The Arabs' broad-mindedness came from more than just religious tolerance. It also served their self-interest because Islamic states had a special tax for non-believers. Therefore, Muslim domains profited by not rushing religious conversions.

The Defense of Constantinople

The Arabs swept the Middle East and North Africa, but their conquest failed at one key place. Twice Muslim armies tried to take Constantinople, so as to open up a route into eastern Europe. Both times the Byzantines held the city.

In the first Muslim attempt in 674 the Arabs attacked by sea but were defeated by the imperial navy wielding one of the world's first secret weapons, a substance called Greek fire. Although its exact nature is now unknown, Greek fire probably contained petroleum. It was pumped into bronze lion heads mounted on warships and then shot across the water to set enemy vessels on fire. It was a fearsome

Heraclius successfully fought the Persians in A.D. 627 only to suffer numerous subsequent losses to invading Arabs.

The Defense of Constantinople

In 717 Constantinople was besieged by an Arab, or Saracen, army and navy. Emperor Theodosius III was forced to abdicate because the army did not trust him, and his place was taken by Leo III, as described in the following excerpt by the ninth-century Byzantine historian Nikephoros, reprinted in Nikephoros, Patriarch of Constantinople.

"The Saracens advanced on the Imperial City itself, sending forth on land an innumerable host of horse and foot [soldiers] recruited from the various people subject to them, as well as a great fleet numbering as many as eighteen hundred ships. . . . When the military and civil dignitaries became aware of these matters, taking account of Theodosius's lack of experience and his incapacity of offering resistance to the enemy, they pressed him with exhortations to abdicate the imperial office and assume without harm a private station. He accordingly withdrew after a reign of one year. Thereupon they held a ballot of who was to become emperor and elected Leo.

The emperor embarked on biremes [warships] and, after breaking the enemy's line, burned [many of] their ships. The remainder of the Saracen fleet, after sailing up the Bosporus, put in at the harbor of Sosthenion and wintered there. That winter happened to be very severe and so much snow fell that the ground was made invisible for a hundred days. Consequently, the Saracens lost no small number of men, horses, camels, and other animals. When spring had come, another great Saracen fleet arrived from Egypt, [and] a short time thereafter yet another fleet came up from Africa. . . . The emperor sent out fire-bearing ships against those fleets and burned all their vessels.

The entire Saracen armament, both cavalry and fleet, withdrew from the Imperial City."

The Byzantines fought off Arab attackers in A.D. 674 using a weapon known as Greek fire, which may have been burning petroleum.

Treaty with Persia

The Byzantine and Persian Empires went to war many times and signed a number of peace treaties over the centuries. The following, excerpted from the sixth-century History of Menander the Guardsman, *is an example of such a treaty and shows that these ancient states had much the same concerns as modern nations.*

"The Persians shall not allow . . . barbarians access to the Roman Empire, nor shall the Romans either in that area or any other part of the Persian frontier send an army against Persia.

Ambassadors and all others using the public [roads] to deliver messages, both those traveling to Roman and those to Persian territory, shall be honored each according to his status and rank and shall receive the appropriate attention.

It is agreed that Saracen [Arab] and all other barbarian merchants of either state . . . shall not cross into foreign territory without official permission.

If anyone during the period of hostilities defected either from the Romans to the Persians or from the Persians to the Romans and if he should give himself up and wish to return home, he shall not be prevented from so doing.

Those who complain that they have suffered some hurt at the hands of subjects of the other state shall settle the dispute equitably, meeting at the border either in person or through their own representatives before the officials of both states, and in this manner the guilty party shall make good the damage."

---

weapon in the Middle Ages because it caught fire when exposed to air and, like all petroleum products, could not be put out with water. With Greek fire the Byzantine navy was able to set much of the Muslim fleet aflame.

In 717 the Arabs made their final bid to take the Byzantine capital. Again they were repulsed, this time by the inspired defense of Emperor Leo III. Durant notes:

An army of 80,000 Arabs and Persians . . . besieged Constantinople from the rear. At the same time the Arabs fitted out a fleet of 1800 vessels . . . ; this armada entered the Bosporus. [Leo positioned] the small Byzantine navy with tactical skill, and saw to it that every ship was well supplied with Greek fire. In a little while the Arab vessels were aflame, and nearly every ship in the great fleet was destroyed. The Greek army made a sortie upon the besiegers, and won so decisive a victory that [the Muslims] withdrew to Syria.[38]

Defender of the West

Although the Byzantines did not fight with this purpose in mind, by battling the Avars and, more important, the Muslims, they protected western Europe from these invaders. Instead of spreading westward, the Avars turned south toward Constantinople. There, they wore themselves out in their unsuccessful attempts to capture the Byzantine capital.

The Muslims, too, slammed hard against the unbreakable defenses of Constantinople. Ostrogorsky points out that "the Byzantine capital was the last dam left to withstand the rising Muslim tide. The fact that it held saved not only the Byzantine Empire, but the whole of European civilization."[39]

The only Muslim conquest in western Europe was that of the Visigothic kingdom of Spain. The remaining military energies of the Arabs went into their protracted conflict with the Byzantine Empire, a war that eventually drained their will to continue fighting. By the end of the ninth century the Arab states were militarily in decline and consequently no longer posed a threat to Europe.

For a century and a half after the death of Justinian I, the Byzantine Empire faced one powerful enemy after another. Although by the beginning of the eighth century it had lost a significant portion of its territory, the empire had survived. Wealth still flowed into it from trade, and its military remained strong. The empire would need both its money and its soldiers as it faced new enemies in the next two centuries.

Chapter Six

Threats from Within: Heretics and Landlords

Peace continued to elude the Byzantine Empire even after the end of aggressive Muslim expansion in the seventh century. The Byzantines had to fortify the empire's eastern borders to discourage Muslim encroachment and also fight the Slavs who were now settled in the Balkans. At the same time the empire was once more troubled by internal conflict caused by religious division and by a shift in power from the emperor to powerful landholders.

The Byzantines and the Slavs

Throughout the eighth century the empire adjusted to the presence of the Slavs in the Balkans. The Slavs posed a unique problem for the empire because, unlike previous invaders, even the Germans, the Slavs were permanent settlers. Out of these Slav settlements would eventually grow kingdoms with whom the Byzantines had to contend.

The Byzantines' defeat of the Muslims at Constantinople in 674 so impressed the Slavs that some of the barbarian tribes sent representatives to the emperor, accepting his authority. Still, on-again, off-again fighting continued with the remainder of the Slavs.

The Bulgarian Kingdom

Much of this fighting arose from conflict with the Bulgarian Kingdom, the first Slavic state. Located in the northeast Balkans, this kingdom sprawled north and south of the Danube.

Although historians consider the Bulgarian domain the first Slavic kingdom, its original rulers were not Slavs but Bulgars, Asian nomads who entered the Balkans in 680. However, the kingdom's Slavic population vastly outnumbered the Bulgar ruling class. During the next century the two groups mixed so thoroughly that the Bulgar minority was assimilated into the Slavic majority.

The Bulgarian Kingdom mounted numerous attacks on the Byzantine Empire, and in 811 the Byzantine emperor Nicephorus I led an army north to deal with the barbarians. The Bulgars destroyed the imperial troops and killed Nicephorus. Two years later the Bulgars struck at Constantinople, but like the Arabs, could not break through the city's defenses.

Taming the Slavs

After its failure to take Constantinople, the Bulgarian Kingdom established more peaceable relations with the empire. Byzantine traders soon found a good market in this kingdom, selling the barbarians everything from crop seeds and plows to gold jewelry and silk. Byzantine architects even went north to design and erect buildings for Bulgarian rulers.

Byzantine teachers brought books and art to the Slavs, and the Byzantine emperors saw to it that, whenever possible, the sons of Bulgarian leaders were educated in Constantinople. When these students returned to their home, they brought with them a taste for Byzantine civilization. Peace with the empire was the only way for these men to have continued access to Byzantine luxuries and learning.

Eventually, Slavic ways and customs gave way to Byzantine manners, and although the empire did not officially control the Bulgarian Kingdom, its influences created a Byzantine culture there. Runciman writes of the Bulgarian Kingdom, "[Tenth-century Bulgarian ruler Symeon,] chief patron of the new culture, had been

Byzantine Emperor Nicephorus I crowns the Bulgar King Michael I Rangabes in A.D. 811.

educated at Constantinople, where he read [deeply]. . . . At his court translators flocked to render Greek chronicles, homilies and romances into the Slavonic; his buildings in his vast capital of Preslav the glorious copied and ambitiously emulated the splendors of Constantinople."[40]

In further imitation of the Byzantine state Symeon dubbed himself an emperor and the Bulgarian Kingdom an empire.

The Slavs and Christianity

The Byzantines successfully used the same nonmilitary tactics in other Slavic states, such as Serbia. Additionally, the empire had another influential tool in controlling the Bulgarians and Slavs: In the ninth century Byzantine missionaries began converting the Slavs to Christianity. Religion became the Byzantine Empire's strongest tie to the barbarians.

In the conversion of the Slavs the Byzantines found themselves competing with western Church missionaries. In the end both branches of the Church were established among the Slavs, more or less according to geographical proximity. Thus, the Byzantines won Slavic converts living in the central and eastern Balkans and Russia, while the Romans gained Slavic adherents in central Europe and the northwestern Balkans.

It was not unusual for neighboring Slavic kingdoms to belong to different branches of the Church. For example, Serbia and Croatia were culturally divided because the Serbs accepted Byzantine Christianity and the Croats, Roman. The different Church loyalties of the two kingdoms affected their relationship, and they became bitter rivals in the region well into the modern age.

Iconoclasm

The Byzantines were diverted from making religious inroads in the Balkans by a new, bitter argument over acceptable Christian practice. Throughout much of the eighth century imperial officials from the emperor down, as well as ordinary citizens, focused their attention on the latest religious controversy, the movement known as iconoclasm.

Iconoclasm, which means the breaking of images, was a belief that holy statues and painted images, or icons, of the Virgin Mary, Christ, and the various saints were sinful. Such icons were to be found in almost every Byzantine church, monastery, shop, and house. The iconoclasts interpreted the presence of icons as a practice that smacked of ancient Greek and Roman idol worship and as a violation of the biblical commandment delivered by God to Moses, "Thou shalt not make unto thee any graven images," and the New Testament verse, "God is a spirit: and they that worship him must worship him in spirit."[41]

Rioting and Repression

In 726 the Byzantine emperor Leo III forbade the use and display of icons. This imperial act enraged the monasteries, whose monks were firm believers in icons. Egged on by angry monks, mobs attacked soldiers removing icons.

Civil war erupted when rebels in favor of icons declared their independence from Constantinople. Each side accused the

Iconoclasm

In the eighth century Byzantine society was divided over iconoclasm, whose followers claimed that holy icons were sinful. In the two excerpts that follow, both quoted in The Eagle, the Crescent, and the Cross, *edited by Charles T. Davis, the argument for icons comes from St. John of Damascus's 742 book* The Fount of Wisdom *and that against them comes from a decree issued by a 754 Church council.*

"Since some find fault with us for worshipping and honoring the image of our Savior and that of our Lady, and those, too, of the rest of the saints and servants of Christ, let them remember that [the story of Christ was] written for the remembrance and instruction of us who were not alive at that time in order that though we saw not, we may still, hearing and believing, obtain the blessing of the lord. But seeing that not everyone has a knowledge of letters nor time for reading, the [Church] Fathers gave their sanction to depicting these events on images."

"God sent his own Son, who turned us away from error and the worshipping of idols, and taught us the worshipping of God in spirit. . . . [The supporters of icons] gradually brought back idolatry under the appearance of Christianity. As then Christ armed his Apostles against the ancient idolatry . . . , so has he awakened against the new idolatry his servants our faithful Emperors.

The painter, who from sinful love of gain depicts that which should not be depicted [and] tries to fashion that which should be believed in the heart. [He has] in his representation . . . depicted the Godhead which cannot be represented."

Followers of iconoclasm believed that holy icons were sinful and sought to destroy them.

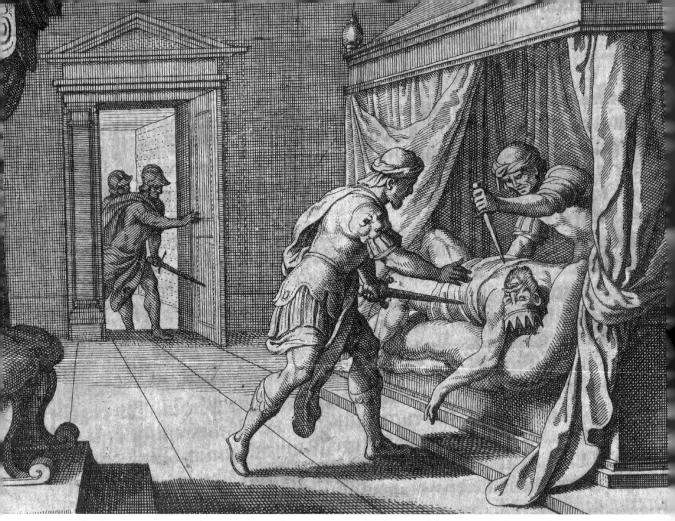

Macedonian Emperor Basil I assassinated Emperor Michael III and became sole leader of the Byzantine Empire.

other of heresy. The rebels organized and launched a fleet, which was sunk along with their cause by the imperial navy, whose victory once more hinged on its use of Greek fire.

The next two emperors were also iconoclasts. One was Leo's son, Constantine V, a particularly brutal enforcer of the icon ban. Constantine had thousands of icons destroyed and ordered the torture, mutilation, and execution of their owners.

Despite such drastic persecution, support for icons remained widespread among both the clergy and general population. Unable to make any significant headway against this majority, the iconoclastic movement gradually lost momentum. Its supporters shrank in numbers, and its political clout diminished accordingly. In 843 a Church council under Emperor Michael III ruled in favor of the display of religious images and thus put an end to iconoclasm.

The Powerful and the Macedonians

More internal trouble, however, lay ahead for the empire. A new political group, known as the Powerful, arose during the last half of the ninth century. The Powerful were landholders who built huge estates, sometimes through the purchase of land, sometimes through its theft. These landowners and the emperors were soon locked in a struggle for control of the empire.

The emperors who opposed the Powerful are known as the Macedonian dynasty. The first Macedonian emperor was Basil I, who like Justinian I had been born a peasant. In 843, after spending much of his youth as a Bulgarian slave, the twenty-five-year-old Basil escaped and reached Constantinople. An intelligent and ruthless man, the former slave rose rapidly from diplomat's groom to coemperor with Michael III. In 867 Basil assassinated Michael to become sole emperor.

Basil I proved to be a capable ruler. He introduced legal and social reforms, restored military strength, and sponsored a new golden age of art and architecture. When he died in 886 the Byzantine state was almost as powerful as it had been under Justinian I. Constantinople had even more trade, more wealth, and more prestige, if not more territory, than during Justinian's reign.

The Battle for Power

However, this prosperity was soon threatened by the struggle between Basil's successors and the Powerful. In the tenth century the great landholders gained control of much of the imperial army by grabbing up land in the military themes. Thus the very soldiers who had once given their loyalty to the emperor were now pledged to support the landlords. The Macedonian emperors could depend only upon the troops they had stationed in and around Constantinople. These imperial troops spent a great deal of their time putting down revolts by the Powerful and their large private armies.

In 976 Basil II came to the throne and passed laws aimed squarely against the Powerful, breaking up a number of the largest estates. However, after his death in 1025 the landowners managed to force the new emperor, Constantine VIII, to repeal these laws.

Zoë and Theodora

In 1034 the management of the empire fell to the two daughters of Constantine VIII, Zoë and Theodora, who inherited the throne when Constantine died without sons or naming a successor. The sisters could do nothing about the Powerful, but they handled other imperial affairs well. For instance, the two were judges in the highest imperial court, and their rulings were famed for their fairness.

Zoë and Theodora were particularly good at exposing corrupt imperial officials. According to Durant, "Seldom had the Empire been better ruled. The imperial sisters attacked corruption in state and Church, and forced officials to disgorge their embezzled hoards; one who had been chief minister surrendered 5300 pounds [2403kg] of gold . . . ; and when

Basil II

The late tenth-century emperor Basil II was a perfect example of the all-powerful emperor whose word was law, as is seen in this description by the eleventh-century Byzantine historian Michael Psellus from his Chronographia.

"[As Basil] grew older and became more experienced he relied less on the judgment of men wiser than himself. He alone introduced new measures, he alone disposed his military forces. As for civil administration, he governed not in accordance with the written laws, but following the unwritten dictates of his own intuition, which was most excellently equipped by nature for the purpose.

Outbursts of wrath he controlled, and like the proverbial 'fire under the ashes,' kept anger hid in his heart, but if his orders were disobeyed in war, on his return to the palace, he would kindle his wrath and reveal it. Terrible then was the vengeance he took on the miscreant. . . . He was slow to adopt any course of action, but never would he willingly alter the decision, once it was taken. Consequently, his attitude toward friends was unvaried, unless by perchance he was compelled by necessity to revise his opinion of them. Similarly, when he burst out in anger against someone, he did not quickly moderate his wrath. Whatever estimate he formed, indeed, was to him an irrevocable and divinely inspired judgment."

In this illustration, the triumphant Basil II stands over conquered Bulgarian chiefs.

the [Constantinople] Patriarch Alexis died, a cache of 100,000 pounds [45,336kg] of silver . . . was discovered in his rooms."[42]

The sisters' personal relations were not always so well managed. In 1042 Zoë became so jealous of her sister's power that she exiled Theodora to a convent. Thirteen years later, after Zoë's death, Theodora left the convent and ruled alone for the last year of her life.

The Church Divided

Near the end of Zoë and Theodora's rule the fragile bond between the Byzantine and Roman factions in the Church broke permanently, driven apart by conflict over doctrine. The eastern Church leaders believed that priests should marry, Rome did not. The eastern leaders claimed that the Holy Spirit came only from God; Rome insisted that it arose from both God and Christ. The Byzantines approved the sacramental use of leavened bread, which includes ingredients to make it rise; Rome did not.

The fighting over these and other matters could not be resolved. In 1052 news reached the patriarch of Constantinople, Michael Cerularius, that Pope Leo IX in Rome had forbidden the use of leavened bread in Byzantine churches in southern Italy. Cerularius, a former high government official with a hard-nosed approach to challenges to his authority, countered by closing Roman churches in Constantinople.

In 1054 a high-ranking Roman bishop, Cardinal Humbert, arrived in Constantinople to meet with Patriarch Cerularius. Humbert was, as Cantor notes, "not the man to be cautious or subservient in his negotiations."[43] Indeed, this short-tempered, unbending representative of the pope would accept only one response from Cerularius: He must give in to the will of Rome. However, the patriarch had no intention of submitting to the pope. In the end the enraged cardinal excommunicated the patriarch—that is, banished him from the Church—and stormed out of the Byzantine capital. Cerularius in turn excommunicated the cardinal, and the rupture was essentially final.

Empire in Trouble

Nothing could be done by the immediate successors of Zoë and Theodora to heal the rupture of the Church. Indeed, the next

Empress Zoë was one of the two daughters of Constantine VIII.

several Byzantine rulers were a weak lot who were unable to manage internal Byzantine affairs, let alone an international crisis. Largely incompetent, they failed to stop a renewed growth of imperial corruption or counter the threat of the Powerful.

One result of this inept leadership was the decline of the Byzantine military. The parts of the imperial army and navy not in the hands of the Powerful were reduced to skeleton forces, and the money intended to buy equipment and to pay soldiers and sailors went into the pockets of imperial officials.

Without an effective military the empire was once more in peril. It lost its territory in Italy to Norman invaders from France, who began their conquest of Sicily and southern Italy in 1060. The Normans captured the last imperial Italian outpost, the seaport of Bari, in 1071.

The empire was also in jeopardy in the East. A new group of Muslims, the Seljuk Turks, had appeared in Asia Minor at about the same time as the Normans in Italy. In 1071 the Turks defeated an impe-

Indictment of the Powerful

In the following indictment, quoted in Crane Brinton's History of Civilization, *the late tenth-century emperor Basil II accuses particular landowners, among others known as the Powerful, who have become rich by stealing land.*

"Constantine Maleinos and his son the magistrate Eustathius have for a hundred years, or perhaps even for a hundred and twenty, been in undisputed possession of lands unjustly acquired. It is the same with the Phocas family, who from father to son, for more than a century, have also succeeded in holding onto lands wrongly obtained. In more recent times certain newly rich men have done the same. For example, Philokales, a simple peasant who lived for a long while in poverty . . . now has [illegally] acquired vast estates. He has not gone unpunished. When we [Basil II] arrived in the region where his property is located, and heard the complaints of those whom he had dispossessed we commanded that all the buildings he had built be razed and that the lands [stolen] from the poor be returned to them. Now this man is living again on the small piece of property which he owned at the start of his career, and has once more become what he was by birth, a simple peasant. Our imperial will is that the same should happen to all those of our subjects, whether of noble birth or not, who have in this way seized the land of the poor."

rial army at Manzikert and captured Emperor Romanus IV.

Alexius I

Romanus abdicated not long after his loss at Manzikert, but the next two emperors were no more successful at stopping the Turks from conquering large sections of Asia Minor than he had been. Then in 1081 one of the Powerful seized the imperial throne, becoming Alexius I. The new emperor faced a situation almost as grim as Heraclius in the seventh century. After throwing the Byzantines out of Italy, the Normans had crossed the Adriatic Sea and invaded the Balkans, and the Turks were still moving steadily across Asia Minor toward Constantinople. To counter these threats, Alexius had a government and army, according to Durant, "crippled with treason, incompetence, corruption, and cowardice."[44]

Alexius hastily tried to rebuild the imperial army with money seized from the Eastern Orthodox Church. Then in 1082 he made an agreement with the Italian city-state of Venice to supply warships to use against the Normans. In exchange for the ships the emperor gave Venice trading rights in the empire. He also sent agents to Sicily to stir up trouble between the Italian population and their Norman overlords. In the end, the Normans were forced to retreat to Italy.

Emperor Alexius Comnenus I sought to unite eastern and western Christians to fight the Muslim Turks.

Alexius I still had to deal with the Seljuk Turks, and again he sought help from the west. He proposed to the Roman Catholic Church that eastern and western Christians combine forces and launch a holy war against the Muslim Turks. By bringing western Europeans into imperial affairs, Alexius set the stage for a disaster that would ultimately be the undoing of the Byzantine Empire.

Chapter Seven

Crusaders and Turks

Beginning at the end of the eleventh century, thousands of western Europeans swarmed into the Byzantine Empire. They came to fight the Seljuk Turks in religious war and to seek their fortunes through trade or service in the imperial government. Conflicts between these foreign adventurers and the Byzantines would plague the empire in its last centuries and would eventually leave the empire too weak to fend off its last enemies, the Ottoman Turks.

Holy War

Trade and war first brought the westerners to the Byzantine Empire. Venetian merchants established themselves in Constantinople and other Byzantine cities under the trade agreement made between Venice and Emperor Alexius I. And, in answer to Alexius's call for help against the Seljuk Turks, even more westerners marched into the empire.

After their victory at Manzikert the Seljuks continued advancing, overrunning more Byzantine territory in Asia Minor. They also defeated their fellow Muslims, the Arabs, winning control of the Middle East, including Palestine and the city of Jerusalem. By 1090 the Turks were the dominant force in the East.

The Byzantines were too weak militarily to fight the Seljuks alone. Consequently, in 1095 Alexius I sought aid from the Roman Catholic Church arguing that eastern and western Christians should join together in a holy war, or crusade, and push the non-Christian Seljuks out of Asia Minor.

Pope Urban II agreed to cooperate with Alexius and called for western Europeans to join the Byzantines in fighting the Turks in a religious campaign known as the First Crusade. Urban hoped first that a joint east-west war against Muslims might reunite the Christian Church. The pope also believed such a crusade could free from Muslim rule not only Asia Minor but also the Christian Holy Land, including Jerusalem.

The Crusaders

Alexius anticipated perhaps a few hundred soldiers would respond to the pope's call. What the First Crusade brought him instead were several armies from France, Germany, and Italy, totaling some thirty thousand warriors. There was no single authority in command of these western armies; each was independently raised and led by a high-ranking western European noble. Below each of these commanders were lesser nobles, accompanied by their knights and foot soldiers.

The leaders of these armies had plans and ambitions that had little to do with those of Alexius I. The emperor, for example, wanted the lands in Asia Minor returned to the Byzantine Empire and, if possible, to acquire the entire Middle East. The western crusaders wanted to enrich themselves on eastern loot and to carve out kingdoms to rule, as well as claim the Holy Land in the name of the Roman Church.

To safeguard his goals Alexius required each of the crusade's leaders to swear an oath of loyalty to him. He hoped that this act would guarantee that any land in Asia Minor regained by the crusaders would be turned over to the empire and that any new states the westerners might create would be under imperial control. Obtaining these

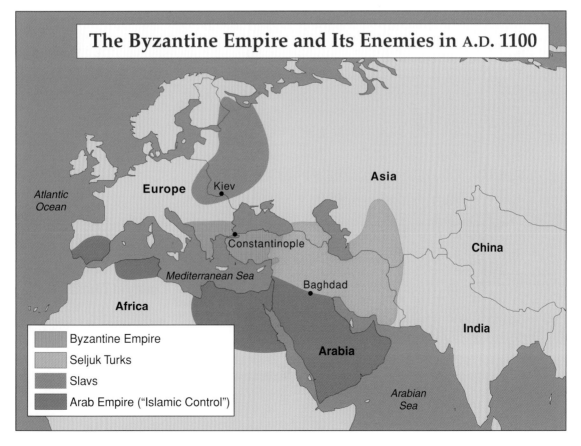

The Byzantine Empire and Its Enemies in A.D. 1100

Atlantic Ocean

Europe

Kiev

Asia

Constantinople

Mediterranean Sea

Baghdad

China

Africa

India

Arabia

Arabian Sea

- Byzantine Empire
- Seljuk Turks
- Slavs
- Arab Empire ("Islamic Control")

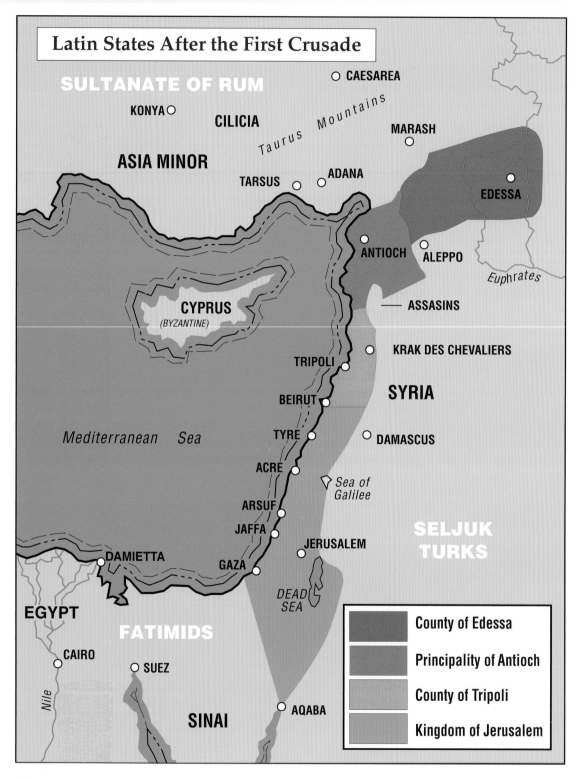

Latin States After the First Crusade

SULTANATE OF RUM

○ CAESAREA

KONYA ○

CILICIA

Taurus Mountains

MARASH ○

ASIA MINOR

TARSUS ○   ADANA ○

EDESSA ○

ANTIOCH ●   ○ ALEPPO

Euphrates

— ASSASINS

CYPRUS
(BYZANTINE)

TRIPOLI ●   ○ KRAK DES CHEVALIERS

SYRIA

BEIRUT ●

Mediterranean   Sea

TYRE ●   ○ DAMASCUS

ACRE ●

◁ *Sea of Galilee*

ARSUF ●

JAFFA ●

SELJUK TURKS

DAMIETTA ●   JERUSALEM ○

GAZA ●

DEAD SEA

EGYPT

FATIMIDS

CAIRO ○

○ SUEZ

Nile

○ AQABA

SINAI

▨	County of Edessa
▨	Principality of Antioch
▨	County of Tripoli
▨	Kingdom of Jerusalem

oaths was not always easy, and Alexius used everything from bribes to withholding food to force them out of the crusaders.

The Crusader States

The crusaders won their first victory against the Turks in 1097 when they captured Nicaea, capital of Turkish Asia Minor. Alexius and the Byzantine army took part in this campaign, but later, while on his way to Antioch, the emperor heard rumors of a large Muslim force headed his way and retreated. The westerners, feeling betrayed, continued the war, moving successfully through Syria and into Palestine, where in 1099 they took Jerusalem.

The reconquered portions of Asia Minor were turned over to the Byzantines, while the victorious crusaders set up four Middle Eastern kingdoms, centered on the cities of Edessa, Antioch, Tripoli, and Jerusalem. The allegiances of these crusader states were not clear, for although Alexius insisted that he had authority over these kingdoms, he had little success in enforcing that authority.

During the twelfth century the Muslims regrouped and began winning back their lost land. In 1144 they took Edessa, and in 1187, Jerusalem. All the remaining crusader kingdoms eventually fell to the Muslims. The Muslim offensive sparked several subsequent western crusades that had varying degrees of success over the next 175 years, but the Byzantines officially had little to do with all but one of these later crusades. This ongoing European activity in the Byzantine world would have important consequences for European culture, however.

The Byzantines and the Latins

After the First Crusade, western Europeans, known to the Byzantines as Latins, were found all over the empire. The Latins did business in Constantinople and served in the imperial army. They even found positions in the government as administrators and diplomats. And they took back to Europe a host of Byzantine goods and ideas that became part of European culture. These included coffee and rice, lemons and apricots, sugar and spices, the game of chess, writing paper, and the Arabic mathematical concept of zero.

The Byzantines and the Latins generally disliked and distrusted one another, however, and relations between them were often strained. The Latins saw imperial citizens as soft, exotic, and treacherous. The Byzantines, on the other hand, thought that the westerners were ill-mannered, savage barbarians and bitterly complained, writes historian Harry J. Magoulias, "of these foreigners, who . . . were ignorant of Greek culture and language."[45] Additionally, both Byzantines and Latins looked on each other as heretics.

Adding to the friction between the Byzantines and the Latins was the empire's increasing dependence upon trade with Venice. The trade alliance that Alexius I had made with Venice gave the Venetians the right to import and export goods without paying customs duties. The merchants of Venice were also exempted from paying taxes and were given an entire section of Constantinople in which to locate their homes, warehouses, and even churches.

A Western View
of the Byzantines

The following account by the twelfth-century historian William of Tyre and reprinted in Harry J. Magoulias's Byzantine Christianity *reveals the western European prejudice against the Byzantines.*

"During the reign of Manuel [1143–1180], beloved of God, the Latins [western Europeans] had found great favor with him—a reward well deserved because of their loyalty and value. The emperor, a great-souled man of incomparable energy, relied so implicitly on their fidelity and ability that he passed over the Greeks [Byzantines] as soft and effeminate and intrusted important affairs to the Latins alone. The Greek nobles, especially the near kindred of the emperor, and the rest of the people as well, naturally conceived an insatiable hatred toward us, and this was increased by the difference between our sacraments and those of their church, which furnished an additional incentive to their jealousy. For they, having separated insolently from the church of Rome, in their boundless arrogance looked upon everyone who did not follow their foolish traditions as a heretic. It was they themselves . . . who deserved the name of heretics, because they had either created or followed new and pernicious beliefs contrary to the Roman church. . . . For these and other reasons they had for a long time cherished this hatred in their hearts and were ever seeking an opportunity, at least after the death of the emperor, to destroy utterly the hated race of the Latins, both in the city and throughout the entire empire."

Venice took over many of the empire's eastern and western trade routes, and as a result, the Byzantines lost control of their own trade during the first half of the twelfth century. Much of the profit that had once gone to imperial merchants and through their taxes into the imperial treasury now went west to Venice.

The Fourth Crusade

The mutual animosity finally climaxed during the Fourth Crusade, launched in 1201. Although their ultimate goal was Jerusalem, the European crusaders had decided that their best strategy would be to take Egypt and then drive east and north into Palestine. The eighty-year-old doge (duke) Enrico Dandolo of Venice promised the crusaders transport vessels and warships, both for steep prices that required the crusaders to go deeply into debt.

Upon reaching Venice, the crusaders were approached by Alexius Angelus, nephew of Byzantine emperor Alexius III. The imperial nephew offered to pay the crusaders' debt to Venice if they would help him become Byzantine emperor, and the deal was struck.

In the summer of 1203 the armies of the Fourth Crusade landed at Constantinople and attacked the city. Using ladders, the crusaders scaled the walls and began setting fire to houses below. This was enough to make Emperor Alexius III flee the city, taking a large part of the empire's treasury with him. The imperial nephew now entered the city and declared himself Alexius IV, while outside the city walls the crusaders waited for their pay.

The Taking of Constantinople

At first, the citizens of Constantinople accepted Alexius IV and his allies as just another set of characters in the ongoing drama of imperial intrigue. However, when they learned of Alexius's bargain with the crusaders, they were outraged. With the treasury emptied by Alexius III, paying off the Fourth Crusade would mean huge tax increases. Alexius IV was strangled, and a new anti-Latin emperor took his place.

When the crusaders realized that they were not going to be paid, they laid siege to Constantinople in the spring of 1204. This time no great general or able emperor stepped forward to direct the city's defenses. The Byzantine army was at an all-time low. The siege lasted a month, and then the city surrendered.

When Constantinople threw open its gates, the crusaders poured through them. The destruction was enormous, with the crusaders looting the city for three days.

Nicholas writes that "the crusaders burned the entire city, including the imperial library and its irreplaceable manuscripts, carried off thousands of relics and smashed whatever statuary was too big to be easily portable." Nicholas concludes that "the sack of Constantinople was a cultural disaster [because,] although some manuscripts were salvaged, the fact that we have only tiny fragments of the original[s] . . . of Plato, Aristotle, the Greek dramatists and poets testifies to the thoroughness of the conflagration [fire]."[46]

The Classics That Survived

Although many original ancient Greek and Roman works were lost in the 1204 sack of Constantinople, a number did survive and were eventually brought west to Italy by Byzantine teachers and scholars. Durant notes: "[Byzantines] brought Greek manuscripts to South Italy, and restored there a knowledge of Greek letters; Greek [Byzantine] professors . . . left Constantinople, sometimes settled in Italy, and served as carriers of the classic germ; so year by year Italy rediscovered Greece."[47]

The classic texts survived not only in Greek and Latin but also in Arabic translations as well. Muslim scholars, after visiting Constantinople, had translated many ancient classics, and these were available to western Europeans in the libraries of Muslim Spain.

The Latin Empire

The Fourth Crusade, however, was not concerned with cultural legacies. It had conquered an empire—or at least the richest city of that empire—and its members

Crusaders at Constantinople

In the following two accounts, as quoted first in Harold Lamb's The Crusades *and second in L. Sprague de Camp's* Great Cities of the Ancient World, *Anna Comnena, daughter of Byzantine emperor Alexius I, describes her mixed feelings about Bohemund, a Norman with the First Crusade, and her shock at the rudeness of other Crusade leaders.*

"Such a man had never been seen before in the lands of the Romans, for he was marvelous to the sight. . . . His clear blue eyes betokened spirit and dignity, as did his nostrils. A peculiar charm hung around this man, and yet there was something horrible in him. For in the size of his body and the glance of his eye, methinks, he revealed power and savagery. Even his laughter sounded like snorting."

"Now the Frankish [western] Counts are naturally shameless and violent, naturally greedy of money too, and immoderate in everything they wish, and possess a flow of language greater than any other human race. . . . Their speech was very long-winded, and as they had no reverence for the Emperor, nor took heed of the lapse of time, . . . not one of them gave place to those who came after them, but kept on unceasingly with their talk and requests. . . . For one came after the other and not only those who had not been heard during the day, but the same [ones] came over again, always preferring one excuse after another for further talk."

intended to enjoy the fruits of victory. The crusaders' first act was to form the Latin Empire and elect one of their own, Baldwin of Flanders, emperor. Venice claimed for itself the coastal towns and islands that would be the most valuable in conducting trade with the eastern Mediterranean.

But the Latin Empire was a shaky venture from the start. In 1204 the Latin rulers controlled only Constantinople, whose population was openly hostile to the westerners. Further, the former crusaders had almost no money.

Additionally, the Latins were poor diplomats surrounded by many enemy states. To the west and south were imperial lands that resisted Latin conquest. To the north were the aggressive Bulgarians, who attacked their new neighbor in 1205. During this war the Latin emperor Baldwin was captured and killed.

The Empire of Nicaea

To the east was the Latin Empire's greatest foe, the Empire of Nicaea. It was to Nicaea in western Asia Minor that many of the refugees from Constantinople fled. There in 1205 Theodore Lascaris, a relative of the imperial family, established a Byzantine government-in-exile. The exiled patriarch of Constantinople crowned Theodore emperor, making him the legal ruler of all Byzantines.

Unlike the crusader rulers of the Latin Empire, Theodore ruled over a strong government and a sound economy. According to Ostrogorsky, the Byzantine emperor in exile "followed the pattern of old Byzantium in every detail. Administration, civil service and imperial household were revived on the old Byzantine principles. The political and ecclesiastical traditions of the Byzantine Empire, which found their symbolical expression in the persons of the Emperor and the Patriarch, were again renewed."[48]

Retaking Constantinople

In 1214 the Empire of Nicaea declared war on the Latin Empire, but the conflict ended in stalemate. There matters stood for almost half a century. Then in 1259 a new emperor, Michael VIII, won a major battle over the westerners.

Two years later, in July 1261, a small Byzantine army found Constantinople virtually undefended. At the time the two empires had declared a temporary truce, and the Latin emperor and most of his troops were occupied by their siege of an island fortress in the Black Sea. The Byzantines, supposedly only on a scouting mission and despite the truce, promptly invaded and captured the capital. When the Latins in the Black Sea heard the news, they fled the region. Michael VIII entered Constantinople on August 15, thus ending the Latin Empire and restoring the Byzantine Empire.

The Shattered Empire

As Michael VIII and his troops rode into Constantinople, they had their first look at the Byzantine capital. Even a half century after the plundering and looting, the damage done the city had only been partially repaired, and the city was still underpopulated.

As for the rest of the old empire, Michael was only able to reconquer fragments of it. Still, the Byzantine emperor did prevent a new western invasion that was being planned by Charles of Anjou, ruler of the Kingdom of the Two Sicilies. Michael engineered a revolt in Sicily that not only prevented the invasion but also led to Charles's overthrow.

Michael VIII further put an end to Venice's imperial trade monopoly by giving trading rights to another powerful Italian city-state, Genoa. This action set off a fierce rivalry between the two cities, but despite the Byzantine emperor's hopes, it did not end Latin meddling in imperial affairs. Brinton notes that "the Genoese and the Venetians, usually at war with each other, [still] interfered at every turn in the internal affairs of the Empire."[49]

Imperial Shadow

The emperors who followed Michael VIII were no more successful than he in reconquering old imperial lands. They simply lacked the resources. Nicholas observes: "The emperors had less wealth and power than some powerful landed families and churches and thus had to use mercenary soldiers, who were expensive and unreliable. The Byzantine fleet had virtually

Looting Santa Sophia

In 1204 the armies of the Fourth Crusade captured and then sacked Constantinople. The following excerpt, found in Crane Brinton's A History of Civilization, *is the Byzantine historian Nicetas Choniates's eyewitness account of the plundering of the great Church of Santa Sophia by the European crusaders.*

"The images, which ought to have been adored, were trodden under foot! Alas, the relics of the holy martyrs were thrown into filth. . . . They snatched the precious [caskets that contained these relics and, after breaking them up,] thrust into their bosoms the ornaments which decorated these and used the broken remnants for pans and drinking cups. . . . They broke into bits the sacred altar, which was formed of all kinds of precious materials and admired by the whole world, and distributed it among the soldiers as was all the other sacred wealth of so great and infinite splendor.

When the sacred vessels of unsurpassable art and grace and the silver and gold ornaments were to be carried off as booty, they brought up mules and saddle horses inside the church itself. Some of these which were unable to keep their footing on the splendid and slippery pavement were stabbed when they fell, so that the sacred pavement was polluted with blood and filth.

A harlot sat in the Patriarch's seat, singing an obscene song and dancing frequently. They drew their daggers against anyone who opposed them at all."

This painting by Eugene Delacroix depicts the Crusaders taking Constantinople in A.D. 1204.

ceased to exist, and the Empire relied on Italians, mainly Genoese, for transport and naval defense.[50]

Civil wars between rivals for the throne also sapped the empire's already badly drained resources. For the next two centuries the imperial domain included little more than Constantinople and small portions of Asia Minor and the Balkans. The final emperors ruled over a shadow of the old empire, their prestige based on old glories and their capital's historical greatness and undeniably important geographical location.

The Fall of the Empire

In the fourteenth century the empire faced its final foe when a new group of Turks, the Ottomans, came out of Asia and swept across Asia Minor. In 1354 the Turks occupied Gallipoli, their first foothold in the empire's European territory. Nine years later the Ottomans moved their capital from Asia Minor to Adrianople. From there they quickly captured what little imperial land remained outside of Constantinople. The emperors appealed to western Europe for help but received no aid.

The Byzantine emperors managed to keep Constantinople out of Turkish hands for a few more decades through negotiation and treaties with the Ottomans. Emperor John V actually provided military assistance to the Turks during the last half of the fourteenth century. Finally, however, in 1453 the Ottomans moved on Constantinople. The Ottoman leader, Mehmet II, wanted to end this lone holdout to Turkish rule.

The Byzantine emperor, Constantine XI, did what little he could to prepare his city for the coming attack. Repeated requests for help from western Europe brought only a trickle of volunteers. In the end Constantine mustered five thousand Byzantine solders plus another three thousand westerners to meet Mehmet and his one hundred thousand troops.

Even though the city had been captured twice before, it was still a formidable target. Its fortress walls remained strong and its citizens and soldiers faced the Ottomans bravely. For over a month the Turks attacked the city from the land and sea.

Finally, on May 29, 1453, Mehmet launched an all-out attack. The Turks' combined forces hit the city from three sides. The battle raged for hours, but in the end the Turks positioned ladders against the city walls and sent enough soldiers into the city to turn the tide in their favor. Thousands were killed in the fighting, including Constantine XI.

After the Empire

After more than a thousand years the Byzantine Empire was no more. It ended as it began, under the rule of an Emperor Constantine. Yet the empire's influence did not die with the fall of Constantinople. That influence was felt by the Turks, who now controlled the same lands as had the Byzantines. The Ottomans created their own empire, modeled upon the Byzantine, with Constantinople, now dubbed Istanbul, their capital.

And the Byzantine Empire left an incalculable legacy to Europe, providing the

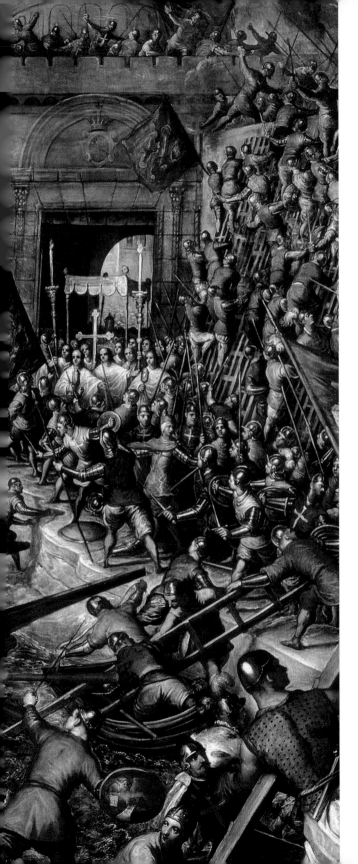

In A.D. 1453, the Ottoman Turks surmounted the walls of Constantinople and seized the city, thereby ending the Byzantine Empire.

ancient Greek and Roman foundation upon which the Western world rests. Ostrogorsky concludes:

> The Byzantine state was the instrument by means of which Graeco-Roman antiquity survived through the ages, and for this reason Byzantium was the donor, the West the recipient. This was particularly true at the time of the Renaissance, when there was such passionate interest in classical civilization and the West found that it could satisfy its longings to explore the treasures of antiquity from Byzantine sources. . . . [The Byzantine Empire] had saved from destruction Roman law, Greek literature, philosophy and learning, so that this priceless heritage could be passed on to the people of western Europe who were now ready to receive it.[51]

Notes

Introduction:
Heirs to the Roman Empire

1. George Ostrogorsky, *History of the Byzantine State*, trans. Joan Hussey, rev. ed. New Brunswick, NJ: Rutgers University Press, 1969, p. 33.
2. Ostrogorsky, *History of the Byzantine State*, p. 33.
3. Will Durant, *The Story of Civilization*, vol. 4, *The Age of Faith*. New York: Simon and Schuster, 1950, p. 4.

Chapter 1:
From Rome to Byzantium

4. Durant, *The Age of Faith*, p. 5.
5. David Nicholas, *The Evolution of the Medieval World: Society, Government and Thought in Europe, 312–1500*. London: Longman, 1992, p. 82.
6. L. Sprague de Camp, *Great Cities of the Ancient World*. Garden City, NY: Doubleday, 1972, p. 426.
7. Crane Brinton, John B. Christopher, and Robert Lee Wolff, *A History of Civilization*, vol. 1, *Prehistory to 1715*, 2nd ed. Englewood Cliffs, NJ: Prentice-Hall, 1960, p. 234.
8. Durant, *The Age of Faith*, p. 43.
9. Norman F. Cantor, *The Civilization of the Middle Ages*. New York: Harper-Collins, 1993, p. 106.

Chapter 2: Shaping the Empire: The Law and the Sword

10. Procopius, *Secret History*, trans. Richard Atwater. Ann Arbor: University of Michigan Press, 1961, p. 67.
11. Durant, *The Age of Faith*, p. 104.
12. Quoted in Aikaterina Christophilopoulou, *Byzantine History*, vol. 1, *324–610*, trans. W.W. Phelps. Amsterdam: Hakkert, 1986, p. 270.
13. Quoted in Brinton, Christopher, and Wolff, *Prehistory to 1715*, p. 226
14. Quoted in Charles T. Davis, ed., *The Eagle, the Crescent, and the Cross: Sources of Medieval History Vol. I c.250–c.1000*. New York: Appleton-Century-Crofts, 1967, p. 115.
15. Christophilopoulou, *Byzantine History*, pp. 312–13.
16. Robert Browning, *Justinian and Theodora*, rev. ed. London: Thames and Hudson, 1987, p. 112.
17. Quoted in Durant, *The Age of Faith*, pp. 109–10.

Chapter 3:
The Byzantine Church and State

18. Quoted in Charles Diehl, *Byzantine Empresses*, trans. Harold Bell and Theresa de Kerpely. London: Elek, 1927, p. 12.
19. Steven Runciman, *Byzantine Civilization*. New York: Barnes and Noble, 1933, p. 109.
20. Durant, *The Age of Faith*, p. 119.
21. Quoted in Tamara Talbot Rice, *Everyday Life in Byzantium*. New York: Barnes and Noble, 1967, p. 62.

22. Brinton, Christopher, and Wolff, *Prehistory to 1715*, p. 227.
23. Runciman, *Byzantine Civilization*, p. 169.
24. Christophilopoulou, *Byzantine History*, p. 220.
25. Ostrogorsky, *History of the Byzantine State*, p. 60.

Chapter 4: The Flowering of Byzantine Culture

26. Brinton, Christopher, and Wolff, *Prehistory to 1715*, p. 224.
27. Durant, *The Age of Faith*, p. 128.
28. Rice, *Everyday Life in Byzantium*, p. 193.
29. Nicholas, *The Evolution of the Medieval World*, p. 91.
30. Quoted in Durant, *The Age of Faith*, p. 121.
31. Runciman, *Byzantine Civilization*, p. 186.
32. De Camp, *Great Cities of the Ancient World*, pp. 430–31.
33. Quoted in Brinton, Christopher, and Wolff, *Prehistory to 1715*, p. 216.

Chapter 5: Threats from Without: The Armies of Persia and Islam

34. Ostrogorsky, *History of the Byzantine State*, p. 82.
35. Durant, *The Age of Faith*, p. 424.
36. Brinton, Christopher, and Wolff, *Prehistory to 1715*, pp. 236–37

37. Ostrogorsky, *History of the Byzantine State*, p. 98.
38. Durant, *The Age of Faith*, p. 425.
39. Ostrogorsky, *History of the Byzantine State*, p. 125.

Chapter 6: Threats from Within: Heretics and Landlords

40. Runciman, *Byzantine Civilization*, p. 225.
41. John 4:24 RSV.
42. Durant, *The Age of Faith*, p. 430.
43. Cantor, *The Civilization of the Middle Ages*, p. 354.
44. Durant, *The Age of Faith*, p. 431.

Chapter 7: Crusaders and Turks

45. Harry J. Magoulias, *Byzantine Christianity: Emperor, Church and the West*. Detroit: Wayne State University Press, 1970, pp. 140–41.
46. Nicholas, *The Evolution of the Medieval World*, pp. 270–75.
47. Durant, *The Age of Faith*, p. 443.
48. Ostrogorsky, *History of the Byzantine State*, pp. 427–28.
49. Brinton, Christopher, and Wolff, *Prehistory to 1715*, p. 367
50. Nicholas, *The Evolution of the Medieval World*, p. 442.
51. Ostrogorsky, *History of the Byzantine State*, p. 572.

For Further Reading

Books

James Barter, *A Travel Guide to Medieval Constantinople.* San Diego: Lucent, 2003. Detailing the weather, money, lodging, entertainment, important structures and cultural centers, and people, this volume allows readers to experience the sights, sounds, smells, and tastes of eleventh-century Constantinople.

———, *World History: The Late Middle Ages.* San Diego: Lucent, 2005. This history tells the story of the last five centuries of the Middle Ages and is filled with instructive illustrations. It contains excerpts from period documents, maps, a time line, and a reading list.

Cherese Cartlidge, *History's Great Defeats: The Crusades: Failed Holy Wars.* San Diego: Lucent, 2002. Relying on first-hand accounts, this title looks at the history and legacy of the crusades.

James A. Corrick, *World History: The Early Middle Ages.* San Diego: Lucent, 2005. Filled with illustrations, this book traces the history of Europe from the fall of Rome to the beginning of the Late Middle Ages. It also contains excerpts from period documents, maps, a time line, and a reading list.

Phyllis Corzine, *World History: The Islamic Empire.* San Diego: Lucent, 2004. This title traces the history of the Islamic world from its beginning through the

twelfth century. It relies on both period and scholarly writings to examine the literary, artistic, and scientific achievements of Islamic society.

Jennifer Lawler, *Encyclopedia of the Byzantine Empire.* Jefferson, NC: McFarland, 2004. In over fifteen hundred entries this work deals with every aspect of the Byzantine Empire and includes lists of emperors, maps of the empire at various stages, and photographs of Byzantine buildings and art.

Tim McNeese, *Sieges That Changed the World: Constantinople.* Broomall, PA: Chelsea House, 2003. This title tells the story of the last days of the Byzantine Empire and the final siege of Constantinople that ended the empire.

Don Nardo, *History's Great Defeats: The Fall of the Roman Empire.* San Diego: Lucent, 2004. This study explores the reasons for the decline and fall of Rome over the course of three centuries and includes a detailed look at the barbarian invasions.

———, *Life During the Great Civilizations: The Byzantine Empire.* San Diego: Blackbirch, 2005. This book describes everyday life in the Byzantine Empire from that of the emperor to farm workers.

———, *Life During the Great Civilizations: Persian Empire.* San Diego: Blackbirch, 2003. This volume presents an intimate look at the lives of the people of the Persian Empire, the great rival of the Byzantine state. It describes the transportation, agriculture, housing, communication, religion, innovation and technology, and social organization of the Persians.

Web Sites

Explore Byzantium (byzantium.seashell. net.nz). This site offers a number of articles on aspects of Byzantine society, as well as useful maps and images of Byzantine art.

Internet Medieval Sourcebook (www. fordham.edu/halsall/sbook.html). This site links to many Byzantine documents, most of which are modern translations.

The Net's Educational Resource Center (members.aol.com/teachernet). This useful site provides links to Byzantine overviews, terms, maps, time lines, daily life, culture, and beliefs.

Works Consulted

Books

Ammianus Marcellinus, *The Roman History of Ammianus Marcellinus.* Trans. C.D. Yonge. London: Bell, 1911. This fourth-century history is packed with information, much of it firsthand, about both the eastern and western Roman empires.

Crane Brinton, John B. Christopher, and Robert Lee Wolff, *A History of Civilization.* Vol. 1, *Prehistory to 1715.* 2nd ed. Englewood Cliffs, NJ: Prentice-Hall, 1960. The chapters on the Byzantine Empire give a good, balanced account of the internal and external struggles of the empire.

Robert Browning, *Justinian and Theodora.* Rev. ed. London: Thames and Hudson, 1987. This in-depth study of the age of Justinian sketches in the character of the important people of the time and looks in detail at the emperor's policies, legal reform, wars, and building programs.

Norman F. Cantor, *The Civilization of the Middle Ages.* New York: HarperCollins, 1993. This thorough history of the Middle Ages by an eminent medieval scholar provides facts and insights into the people and events important to Byzantine history.

Aikaterina Christophilopoulou, *Byzantine History.* Vol. 1, *324–410.* Trans. W.W. Phelps. Amsterdam: Hakkert, 1986. This history by an eminent scholar offers a thorough look at the first three centuries of the Byzantine Empire, from the founding of Constantinople to the reign of the Heraclius emperors.

Charles T. Davis, ed., *The Eagle, the Crescent, and the Cross: Sources of Medieval History*, Vol. I *c. 250–c. 1000.* New York: Appleton-Century-Crofts, 1967. This collection is an excellent source of Byzantine writings. Each Byzantine piece is either by or about a major imperial figure.

Elizabeth Dawes and Norman H. Baynes, trans., *Three Byzantine Saints: Contemporary Biographies.* London: Mowbrays, 1948. This books contains translations of three popular Byzantine saints' lives.

L. Sprague de Camp, *Great Cities of the Ancient World.* Garden City, NY: Doubleday, 1972. The chapter on Constantinople is full of interesting information about the history and growth of the city from the time of Constantine I to the modern day. Photographs and maps complement the text.

Charles Diehl, *Byzantine Empresses.* Trans. Harold Bell and Theresa de Kerpely. London: Elek, 1927. This very readable account describes the lives and political careers of fourteen Byzantine empresses.

Will Durant, *The Story of Civilization.* Vol. 4, *The Age of Faith.* New York: Simon and Schuster, 1950. This classic study of the Middle Ages is written in a readable and accessible style and ends with a large bibliography. Its sections on the Byzantine Empire are filled with facts, incidents, and speculation about the culture.

Michael Grant, *History of Rome.* New York: History Books Club, 1978. This one-volume history provides useful information about the eastern Roman Empire and its transformation into the Byzantine Empire.

Harold Lamb, *The Crusades.* Garden City, NY: Doubleday, 1945. Half of this very readable and informative history of the Crusades deals with the First Crusade, presenting a balanced account of the interactions of the Byzantines and the crusaders.

Liudprand, *The Works of Liudprand of Cremona.* Trans. F.A. Wright. London: Routledge and Kegan Paul, 1930. This collection of writings by a tenth-century western European contains the author's account of his two trips to Constantinople.

Harry J. Magoulias, *Byzantine Christianity: Emperor, Church and the West.* Detroit: Wayne State University Press, 1970. This study examines the nature of the eastern Church and its importance to the development and political goals of the Byzantine Empire.

Menander, *The History of Menander the Guardsman.* Trans. R.C. Blockley. Liverpool, UK: Cairns, 1985. This account by the sixth-century Byzantine historian Menander provides much information on imperial politics and Byzantine relations with Persia and the Avars.

David Nicholas, *"The Evolution of the Medieval World: Society, Government and Thought in Europe, 312–1500.* London: Longman, 1992. This excellent history of the Middle Ages has sections on the Byzantine Empire that show how religion, politics, art, and everyday life contributed to the development of the empire. Each chapter ends with a list of suggested readings, and the book has an excellent map section at the back.

Nikephoros, *Nikephoros, Patriarch of Constantinople: Short History.* Trans. Cyril Mango. Washington, DC: Dumbarton Oaks, 1990. This account by the ninth-century Byzantine churchman Nikephoros details the emperorships of Heraclius and several of his successors. It provides much interesting information about the final Persian war.

George Ostrogorsky, *History of the Byzantine State.* Trans. Joan Hussey. Rev. ed. New Brunswick, NJ: Rutgers University Press, 1969. This classic study of the Byzantine Empire maps out the complex events that took the empire from the time of Constantine I to that of Constantine XI. Many full color maps depict the various gains and losses of the empire.

Procopius, *Secret History.* Trans. Richard Atwater. Ann Arbor: University of Michigan Press, 1961. This famous sixth-century exposé presents a different view of Justinian I and Theodora than found in this writer's official histories.

Michael Psellus, *The Chronographia.* Trans. E.R.A. Sewter. London: Routledge and Kegan Paul, 1953. This eleventh-century chronicle details the final decades of the Macedonian line of Byzantine emperors.

Tamara Talbot Rice, *Everyday Life in Byzantium.* New York: Barnes and Noble, 1967. Full of black-and-white drawings that support descriptions of all aspects of Byzantine life, this volume covers such topics as the emperor and his family, the Church, the military, town and country life, and artists and architects.

David Ricks, *Byzantine Heroic Poetry.* Bristol, UK: Bristol Classical, 1990. This volume provides an informative discussion and translation of the eighth-century *Digenis Akritas*, the most famous Byzantine epic poem.

Steven Runciman, *Byzantine Civilization.* New York: Barnes and Noble, 1933. Each chapter of this classic study looks at a different part of Byzantine culture and society, ending with a discussion of the empire's relations with neighboring states.

Samuel P. Scott, trans., *The Civil Law.* 17 vols. Cincinnati: Central Trust, 1932. This multivolume translation contains the entire Byzantine legal code, as revised by order of the sixth-century emperor Justinian I.

James Stevenson, ed., *Creeds, Councils, and Controversies: Documents Illustrating the History of the Church, AD 337–461.* Rev. W.H.C. Frend. London: SPCK, 1989. This collection of excerpts from early Church writings covers such subjects as the relation of the Church to the empire, Monophysitism, and the pope's supremacy.

Index

Adrianople, 19, 87
Alexandria, 44, 48
Alexius Angelus, 82–83
Alexius I, 77, 78–79, 81, 84
Alexius III, 83
Alexius IV, 83
Ammianus Marcellinus, 20
Anastasius, 24
anchorites, 54
Anna Comnena, 84
Antioch, 44, 48, 81
Arabs. *See* Muslims
architecture, 54–55
Arius, 45–46
army. *See* military
art, 55–58
Attila, 21
Avars, 60, 61, 62

Baldwin of Flanders, 85
Basil I, 73
basilica, 55
Basil II, 73, 74, 76
Baynes, Norman, 53
Belisarius, 27, 30, 32–36
bishops, 42, 43–46
books, 52–54
Brinton, Crane, 21, 42–43, 50, 76, 86
Browning, Robert, 33
Bulgarian Kingdom, 68–70
Bulgars, 68, 85
Byzantine Christianity, 70

Byzantine Christianity (Magoulias), 82
Byzantine Empire, 22, 81
    corruption in, 73–74, 76
    economic strength of, 38, 40–41
    importance of, 12, 67, 89
    invasions of, 61–62
    language of, 17, 29
    legal code of, 27–30
    restoration of, 85–87
    roots of, 10–11
    wars of, 30–36
Byzantium, 11–12

Cantor, Norman F., 22
Carthage, 32
ceremonies, 37, 39, 50
Cerularius, Michael, 75
Chalcedon, 47
Choniates, Nicetas, 86
Christianity, 37, 48, 75
    books of, 52–55
    Slavs and, 70–72
    as state religion, 11, 16, 37, 48, 52
Christophilopoulou, Aikaterina, 30, 47
Chronographia (Psellus), 74
churches, 55–58
Civil Law, The (Justinian I), 31
Code of Justinian, 27–30, 31
coins, 40–41
commerce, 38, 40–41
Constantine I, 12, 14, 16
Constantine V, 72

Constantine VIII, 73
Constantine XI, 87
Constantinople, 15, 16, 44, 67
    destruction of, 83, 84, 86
    naming of, 11–12, 14
Council of Chalcedon, 47, 48
Council of Ephesus, 45, 47
councils, 45–46
Creeds, Councils, and Controversies
    (Stevenson), 45
crusaders, 78–84
crusader states, 81
Crusades, 78–84
Crusades, The (Lamb), 84
culture, 49–50, 52–54

Davis, Charles T., 71
Dawes, Elizabeth, 53
de Camp, L. Sprague, 20, 28, 84
decoration, 55–58
Dioscurus, 45, 47
Durant, Will, 12–13, 15, 21, 25, 38, 40, 50,
    66, 77, 83

Eagle, the Crescent, and the Cross, The
    (Davis), 71
Eastern Orthodox Church, 77
electors, 38
emperor, 37–38, 40, 50
Ephesus, 45, 47

First Crusade, 78–81
Flavian, 47
Fourth Crusade, 82–83, 86

Germans, 18, 21
gold, 40–41
Goths. *See* Ostrogoths; Visigoths
government, 37–38
Grant, Michael, 22

Great Cities of the Ancient World (de
    Camp), 28, 84

Hellenism, 16
Heraclius, 61, 63
heretics, 48
hermits, 54
History of Civilization (Brinton), 76, 86
History of Menander the Guardsman
    (Menander), 66
History of Rome (Grant), 22
History of the Wars (Procopius), 34
Humbert, 75
Huns, 21, 60
Hypatia, 52

iconoclasm, 70–72
icons, 70–72
Islam, 62–67
Istanbul, 15, 87
    see also Constantinople

Jews, 48
jihad, 62–67
John V, 87
Justin I, 24
Justin II, 59
Justinian I
    achievements of, 24, 36
    architectural projects under, 54–55
    conquests of, 30, 32, 33, 34
    taxation and, 27, 30
    wars of, 32, 59
    see also Code of Justinian
Justinian and Theodora (Browning), 34

Lamb, Harold, 84
Later Roman Empire, 11
Latin Empire, 83, 85
laws. *See Code of Justinian;* government;
    emperor

Leo I, 47
Leo III, 70, 72
Leo IX, 75
libraries, 12, 49
Liudprand, 39, 40

Macedonian dynasty, 73
Magoulias, Harry J., 81, 82
Maurice, 50, 60
Mecca, 62
Mehmet II, 87
Menander, 66
Michael III, 72, 73
Michael VIII, 85, 85–86
Milan, 15, 17
military
    decline of, 76–77
    defense of Constantinople by, 64–66
    Justinian's, 30, 32–34, 36, 38, 59
    rebuilding of, 61–62
money, 40–41
monks, 43
Monophysitism, 45–46, 48
mosaics, 55
Muhammad, 62
Muslims, 62–67

Narses, 33
navy. See military
Nicaea, 81
Nicephorus I, 69
Nicholas, David, 18, 52, 83, 86–87
Nika riot, 27, 28, 54
Nikephoros, 63, 65
Nikephoros, Patriarch of Constantiople
    (Nikephoros), 63, 65
Normans, 77
North Africa, 32

Odoacer, 21–23

Ostrogorsky, George, 10, 12, 60–62, 67,
    85, 89
Ostrogoths, 21–23, 33–35
Ottoman Empire, 87–88
Ottoman Turks, 87–89

pagans, 48
Patriarch of Constantinople, 42
Persian Empire, 18, 31–32, 49–50, 61–62,
    66
Phocas, 61, 63
pope, 43–44, 47, 72, 75, 79
Powerful, the, 73, 76
Procopius, 24, 27, 35–36
Psellus, Michael, 74

Ravenna, 17, 22, 33
rebellions, 27, 28, 38, 60–61, 73
    see also Nika riot
religion
    artistic representation of, 55–58
    disputes within, 43–46
    emperor's role in, 41–42
    importance of, 42–43
    see also Christianity; Muslims
Rice, Tamara Talbot, 51–52
rituals, 37, 39, 50
Roman Catholic Church, 77
Roman Christianity, 70
Roman Empire, 10, 17, 18–21, 35
Romanus IV, 77
Rome, 15
Romulus Augustulus, 10, 21
Runciman, Steven, 16, 38, 42–43, 52, 54,
    69–70

Santa Sophia, 55, 59, 86
Saracens. *See* Muslims
schools, 51–52
Secret History (Procopius), 28

Seljuk Turks, 76, 77, 78
senate, 38
Slavs, 60, 68, 68–72
social classes, 29
Stevenson, James, 45
stylites, 54
Symeon, 69–70

teachers, 52
Theodora (daughter of Constantine
    VIII), 73–74
Theodora (wife of Justinian I), 25–27
Theodore, 85
Theodoric, 22–23
Theodotus, 53
Three Byzantine Saints (Dawes and
    Baynes), 53
Tiberius II, 59
trade, 38, 40–41

territories, 17
treaties, 66
Tribonian, 27–28
Turks, 77, 78

Valens, 17, 19
Valentinian I, 17
Vandals, 32
Venice, 81–82, 85
Visigoths, 18–20, 67

wall paintings, 55, 58
William of Tyre, 82
Wolf, Hieronymous, 11
women's rights, 29

Zeno, 21–23
Zoë, 73–74

Picture Credits

Cover, Scala/Art resource, N.Y.

The Art Archive/Bargello Museum, Florence/Dagli Orti, 57 (upper right)

The Art Archive/Biblioteca Capitolare/Dagli orti, 29

akg-images, 19

akg-images/Werner Forman, 39

Werner Forman/Art Resource, N.Y., 13, 53

Giraudon/Art Resource, N.Y., 16, 31

Erich Lessing/Art Resource, N.Y., 8 (lower left), 56 (upper Left), 75, 86

Reunion des Musees Nationaux/Art Resource,N.Y., 51, 63

Scala/Art Resource,N.Y., 9 (lower right), 11, 89-90

Snark/Art Resource,N.Y., 77

The Bridgeman Art Library, 65, 69

© Alinari Archives/CORBIS, 56 (lower right)

© Archivo Iconografico,S.A./CORBIS, 9 (lower left), 25, 26, 44

© Bettmann/CORBIS, 9 (upper)

© Brooklyn Museum of Art/CORBIS, 46-47

© Elio Ciol/CORBIS, 57 (upper left)

© Werner Forman/CORBIS, 41 (right), 42, 74

© Lindsay Hebbard/CORBIS, 57 (lower)

© Milner Moshe/CORBIS, 41 (left)

© Bill Ross/CORBIS, 8 (upper)

© ML Sinibaldi/CORBIS, 18 (lower right)

© Paul A. Souders/CORBIS, 56 (lower left)

© Murat Taner/ZEFA?CORBIS, 56 (upper right)

Hulton Archive by Getty Images, 32, 72

Time-Life Pictures/Getty Images, 34

Mary Evans Picture Library, 33, 40, 45, 50, 64, 71

Steve Zmina, 79

About the Author

James A. Corrick has been a professional writer and editor for twenty-five years. Along with a PhD in English, his academic background includes a graduate degree in the biological sciences. He has taught English, edited magazines for the National Space Society, and edited and indexed books on history, economics, and literature. He and his wife live in Tucson, Arizona. Among his other titles for Lucent are *The Renaissance, The Industrial Revolution, The Civil War: Life Among the Soldiers and Cavalry, The Louisiana Purchase, Life of a Medieval Knight, The Incas, The Civil War, Life Among the Incas*, and *The Early Middle Ages.*